KABULI DAYS
Travels in Old Afghanistan

by *Edward* Field

Kabuli Days: Travels in Old Afghanistan
By Edward Field

Text Copyright © 2008 Edward Field
Book Copyright © 2008 World Parade Books

First Edition

ISBN 10 # 0-9817136-4-5
ISBN 13 # 978-0-9817136-4-9

Cover Photographs: Yusuf Taraki
Cover Design: Dean Tsuyuki
Managing Editor: Paul Kareem Tayyar
Text Editing: Paul Kareem Tayyar and LeeAnne Langton

For Press and Press Contact Information:

Paul Kareem Tayyar
World Parade Books
5267 Warner Avenue #191
Huntington Beach, CA
92649

$\mathscr{P}$aul Kareem Tayyar

Foreword

Though for most the Summer of Love was just that, a fleeting season of bliss and spirit, sound-tracked by electric twelve strings and tambourines played by pretty girls in Golden Gate Park and upstate New York, Edward Field is one of the treasured few who never let that summer die. His poetry—from the verse-form valentines to faded movie stars in *Variety Photoplays* to the playful come-ons to handsome bowery boys in *Counting Myself Lucky*—Field's career has been a sustained resistance to our country's collective surrender—politically, artistically, ethically, sexually—to the safe, the staid, the expected. If America has become defined by an almost crippling socio-cultural conformity, where a race of intellectual wardens and physical autocrats contaminate so much of the society, Field is America's Sundance Kid, its Peter Pan, its Robin Hood: ageless, fearless, playful, iconoclastic, aware that life's beauty is found not in mergers and acquisitions, on-line investment banking, or Club Med vacations financed by a well-managed 401K, but in writing, lovemaking, and, as is the case with *Kabuli Days*, traveling. There are so few true free-spirits left it is easy to forget that there was a time when we thought men like him were going to take over the world: in 1968, for instance, when bands like The Byrds and Crosby, Stills, Nash, and Young were storming the charts with their strummed dream-poems of faith and free love, when Lawrence Ferlinghtetti and Denise Levertov were writing some of their finest lyrics of nature and love and paisley utopias, when films like *Faces* and *Bonnie and Clyde* were playing in first-run theaters in Chicago and Los Angeles. And Field was one of them: a former bomber navigator in World War II who once joked that "the army was the only place he wasn't beaten up for being gay," his conversational poetic style lending an everyman tenor to his note-perfect verses.

But by 1971 it was, as we know, all over. And Field, nearing fifty, a bit too old to call himself a "hippie," as he himself put it, but still sustained by the spark of limitless possibility he holds to this day, saw a photograph in *National Geographic* of a hotel nestled into a riverside mountain in the middle of Afghanistan. He bought a ticket, packed a bag, and off he went, into the land of deserts and poppies, camels and dervishes, shrines and caves, where decades-old buses carried brave passengers over mountains old as the world itself, where threats of a Russian invasion was always on the back of everyone's minds, where women were consigned to a life of near-hermitage, kept out of schools and off of Main Streets, unable to drive or to date whomever they chose, where sending a package back to the states was more difficult than one could ever imagine. In these journals we meet hippies from Berkeley, smoking hash and opium on their way to Katmandu, idealistic Peace Corps workers who may or may not be unwitting imperialist foot soldiers, wealthy, big-hearted German doctors and catty French tourists, all of them ultimately swallowed by a landscape they are incapable of understanding, but who are given the authorial tenderness and love they deserve by our writer.

Though the Middle East of *Kabuli Days* is hardly a paradise—it is too riddled with poverty, too locked into oppressive ideas about religion and sex to be stated as such—that a gay Jewish man could travel (relatively) freely for over a year there is something quite magical; Field is always aware of this is in his travels, though not to the point that he overlooks Afghanistan's almost casual cruelty to women and children, and its seemingly pre-literate standards law and of justice.

Simply put, *Kabuli Days* is a work of enchantment: a journey into a world whose exotic strangeness mirrors the emotional crisis of its creator—and hopefully gives readers a better sense of a country it should know more about, and the people who live there.

Paul Kareem Tayyar
World Parade Books
June 2008

KABULI DAYS
Travels in Old Afghanistan

by *Edward* Field

Introduction

In 1970, not long before the King of Afghanistan was deposed and all the troubles began that led to decades of civil strife and armed conflict, I went there. My personal life was in crisis, and it was the furthest place I could imagine on earth to escape to.

Afghanistan lies deep in that mysterious heartland of central Asia which, we learn in school, sent hordes of barbarians into the West—think Genghis Khan. With our education largely focused on the western Christian world, almost everything beyond is remote and exotic. But by the time I went to Afghanistan, I'd made several visits to Morocco, which lies at one end of the great caravan routes that once extended all the way to China, and my imagination had already opened up to the other, the "forbidden" world.

I decided to go after leafing through a National Geographic in my dentist's office one day and came across pictures of a remote country that attracted me instantly; not so much because of its strangeness, but because there was something familiar about it, something I felt I belonged to. It was Afghanistan. One of the most striking photos was of a little hotel clinging to a rock in the middle of a rushing river, the wild, remote Pamir Mountains around it.

I told some astrologer friends who checked my horoscope for Afghanistan and gave me the cryptic news that I would be a perfectly ordinary person there, so why did I want to go? But that sounded good to me, a place where I wouldn't feel "different." And sure enough, one of the things I found in Afghanistan, once the first shock of its strangeness had passed and I started to understand it a little, was not that I had changed there and become ordinary, as my horoscope suggested, but that I was ordinary there because the men were more like me than anywhere I'd ever been—astonishingly, I had found a land where I was like others. It was not just that men often had long hair like mine, but the idea of a "gentle" man is part of Muslim culture. Men were publicly affectionate in ways that would be looked at askance here. And my sexual preference was not the problematic identity gay men have in the western world, that caused me so much anguish in my earlier life.

But if Afghan men enjoyed more freedom than we do, speaking on a personal level, women paid the price. They were on the order of slaves. Sequestered all their lives, they were sold by fathers and bought by husbands. A popular ballad "Chamoli" said, "Go and tell the darling girl that her lover has come: Flower Eyes, your buyer has come ...Oh God, my heart is sad, for the heart of my darling is like a stone"—as well it might be, since she has been sold to him like a chattel by her father, who has beaten her regularly all her life to make her submissive to this fate.

Things had already improved tremendously for women in Kabul by the time I got there, though they were still hardly visible in daily life—and if a woman was alone on the street after dark for any reason, I was told, she was seen by men as belonging to no one and was fair game. Though foreign women could dress as they pleased in public, and I did see one now and then, Afghan women had to wear the *chadri*, now called a *burqa*, the totally enveloping garment that leaves only a latticework of threads over the eyes to see through. Admittedly, it was attractively pleated and embroidered, and moreover gave a woman freedom in public to nurse a baby underneath, or to squat to pee. In the countryside, as little under control of the central government then as now, not much had changed for women—except that they were no longer being stoned to death for adultery.

It is a pity we hear so little from the woman's point of view about the brief decade under the Soviet Union when they were liberated, at least in the cities, but it seems unlikely that any of the factions now in power is likely to allow serious improvements for women, and certainly no release from their chattel status.

Afghanistan has always been called a crossroads, and most of the foreigners I met there were passing through. These were tourists flying in for a brief stay at one of the two deluxe hotels on a Pan Am round-the-world tour, and then there were the "world travelers," the youth on the move over the land routes from anywhere in Europe, America, and Australia. They stayed at a series of internationally-known hippie hotels that were notable for filth and harassment by police. For most of these, too, Kabul was just a druggie layover before traveling on to India, perhaps to search for a guru, and Katmandu, the ultimate goal for drugs and fantasy.

The rest of the foreigners were the embassy families living in compounds, and the AID missions of various countries, each assigned a different project to work on—for example, irrigation (Chinese), highways (American and Russian), law faculty (American), post office (French), police (the Germans, naturally). There was a tiny liberal Peace Corps presence, mostly teaching English and typing out in the villages. American officials, who were receiving hardship pay for this posting, were downright hostile to us "world travelers" who they felt had no right to be there, and must be out of our minds—or up to no good—to come to such a backward country voluntarily. Of course, nearing fifty I was too old for hippiedom myself, but in their eyes I still fell into the category since I was living the hippie life. The officials themselves were as cut off from the harsh realities we dealt with day to day, and were mostly living in a huge walled suburban-style compound of ranch houses, where they and their families could enjoy all the amenities of home.

It certainly took a lot of traveling to get to such a remote, land-locked country, especially since, instead of flying directly to the capital, Kabul—the easy way—I chose to go overland from Europe through Turkey and Iran. I took the Orient Express to Istanbul, but having heard of the terrible roads in Turkey and how buses even had to drive across river beds, I skipped that part and flew across Turkey from Istanbul to Erzurum in the shadow of Mt. Ararat near the Iranian border. From then on it was buses, share-taxis, sometimes trucks, in day-long and night-long stages, never far from the southern border of the Soviet Union. Traveling by land increases the feeling of distance. But if the shore of the Caspian Sea seemed far away, it was nothing to the far feeling I got when I reached Wakhan, the tip of Afghanistan that touches the Chinese border. It was there, the furthest point of my travels, that I stayed in the guesthouse built on a rock in the middle of a rushing river that I had seen in the National Geographic in the Manhattan dentist's office. In fact, the whole time in Afghanistan I felt like I was in the furthest place on earth, and I never got over the anguish at being so far away—but far from where?

The concept of "home" hit me for the first time. It was like finding myself on some distant planet with no return likely.

Of course, my arrival in Kabul had to be a letdown, with the city enveloped in a cloud of dust, for most of the city was unpaved, and the least wind sent the dust flying. I often tried to describe Kabul but never succeeded and photographs don't show it. Early on, I thought, "the city of Kabul looks like it was bombed out and a few modern buildings have risen from the ruins, which are still being used for shops and living." Another attempt: "I can't send photos of it and can't describe it. The postcard views are all taken from above, from the surrounding hills, so they don't show the place with the hills behind it, which is the way it looks from anywhere in the city. There are always bare mountains with cave-like houses rising up it, almost blending into the rock except for dark squares of doors and windows. The mountains move nearer or farther according to the weather or time of day: The river that cuts through, roughly dividing old Kabul from new, is a stagnant series of dammed up, scummy ponds where people bathe, wash their clothes, and even brush their teeth and drink." And, "Yesterday when a camel train passed me in the market, it struck me again what an unusual city this is. Even in this fancy side of town, men ride by on donkeys, and sheep are herded through the streets...." But from later pages of my diary, "I thought when I arrived that Kabul was dry, hideous, unlivable, but now see it as beautiful and magical." It was so different from anything else, even memories of it don't travel well and are hard to make sense of in my current New York context. But the place it resembles the most to my mind, when I try to summon it up is, perhaps, Taos Pueblo, but without the architectural elegance of the pueblo, if that makes any sense.

At the time I went I was interested in the subject of Sufism, as a result of my interest in the writings of Gurdjieff, one of the few Sufi masters I knew of in the West, who reportedly had gained much of his esoteric knowledge in Central Asia, studying in monasteries in the Hindu Kush, the mountain range that divides the country. So wherever I went in the East, where Sufism is part of life, I asked about dervishes and monasteries. I confess I did not learn very much. But there was a spiritual impact nevertheless. My stay in Afghanistan in some way refocused me, for people there are very different from us, in what I can only call an ancient way, and learning to communicate with them changed me forever. My diary records this change of perception, as well as my initial difficulties in understanding the people. Things got better as I learned the language. Though I never fully entered this ancient, complex society (one half of which, the women, was off limits and shrouded from my eyes), it was a tremendous learning experience.

Although I was on the lookout for sex, as all travelers are, I felt somewhat puzzled by the "signs and portents." For a gay male, sex seemed available all over the place, but I was past the age of desperation, and didn't plunge in where I didn't understand. It was intriguing that there didn't seem to be any categories for sex—gay and straight sex were just accepted as possibilities for male sexuality, what men did. Afghanistan seemed pretty much to follow the mores of other Muslim countries, even where punitive laws, presumably based on the Koran, are on their books.

Since I'd been to Morocco several times, as well as Tunisia, Egypt, and Turkey, the two "purest" and most colorful Muslim lands continued to be Morocco and Afghanistan, strangely, at opposite ends of the old Silk Road. Afghanistan, though, lacked Morocco's French influence, with its lovely architecture, good little hotels, baguettes, restaurants, and cafés. I had an entrée into Morocco's mixed culture, since I was introduced to it by my friend Alfred Chester, who lived there, and I spoke passable French, the second language of Moroccans. But as it turned out, the principal language of Afghanistan, Farsi, did not pose a great challenge. It may be hard to believe that I could have become fluent in this language in the few months of my stay, when Americans, stationed there, generally throw up their hands, even the embassy officials and Aid workers who you'd think would be required to learn it. But Farsi is very much like a European language. Similar words abound, and the syntax is like ours. The colloquial Farsi I learned from talking to ordinary Afghans was simpler than the Iranian version. Iranian Farsi sounds more elegant than Afghan—Iranians seem to talk down their noses, much as standard British speech sounds high falutin' to Americans. I know my Afghani accent was rustic, because on my return through Iran, feeling so proud of myself, the Iranians smiled when I spoke. However, I never succeeded in learning to read the Arabic script, since to adapt it to the Farsi tongue it is augmented with a seemingly infinite number of extra little marks. Actually, the Pashtoo language is also spoken by many Afghans, of whom about half are Pashtoons, and many of the words I learned from them were probably Pashtoo.

The prices for almost everything were extraordinarily low, even miniscule, by western standards, and it may be strange to see me debating between spending a cent and a half on a bus and 25 cents on a gari, a horse-drawn carriage, or complaining at being over-charged 2 Afghanis for tea instead of 1, when there were 70 or 80 to the dollar. I did have more than enough money for the summer, as it turned out, but fell into a trap I tend to fall into in very poor countries—cheap as prices are, I start taking a local attitude toward them and haggle over pennies. But it resulted in my living on the local economy and getting to know the Afghani people, though unlike most of them I always had an escape hatch.

This diary is not a report on the political situation of that time—I knew very little about that, or even the history of the country, I must confess. It is just a record of what I observed as a private person. I did know something about the "Great Game," the competition between Russia and Britain to control Central Asia, with their spies that fed the paranoia of the region, but I blanked out before the complications of the age-old "Pashtoonian Question," which I gathered was similar to the Kurdish struggle or the Macedonian, where the people were divided up between different countries when borders were drawn, causing difficulties for the nomadic tribes that populate much of the region.

From all reports I read, the people and the customs and the landscape have remained pretty much the same as when I visited there, though the country has meanwhile suffered the greatest devastation since Genghis Khan swept through 800 years ago. And peace is not yet in sight.

At the end of the summer, my return to the "outside" world was a series of revelations, and in Tehran I was struck with amazement at the kiosks and bookstores with newspapers and books. In Afghanistan, I hardly ever saw anyone reading—indeed, it was a pre-literate culture and the people were largely illiterate. Therefore, during a previous campaign against the Taliban, when American airplanes dropped leaflets along with food supplies to the people, it only showed how ignorant our government was of the country we were trying to help—no one could read them!

I was also dreadfully sick when I returned from Afghanistan—though I'd become terribly gaunt and thin, and had somehow escaped amoebic dysentery, I was suffering from a deep bronchial infection, and by some instinct of self-preservation headed for Israel, a country with a modern healthcare system.

I learned a lot about myself in Afghanistan, in fact I have pondered my experiences there ever since, but I would never go back, for it is the most difficult place I have ever been to, with its harsh landscape that demands a great deal of rigor and fortitude. Still, though I never stopped suffering over my problems at home, I constantly felt throughout my summer in Afghanistan that it was possible to wake up there one morning and be happy.

After the long and arduous journey across eastern Europe, Turkey and Iran, I arrived at the town of Mashad on the eastern border of Iran, the jumping-off place for Afghanistan, where I got my visa. Across the Afghan border is the city of Herat, and on the morning I left Mashad by bus, Herat was to be my first stop on the road to Kabul. Little did I know that the two-hundred mile journey would take fifteen hours....

JUNE 19. Mashad, Iran. With my visa for Afghanistan, I'm at the bus terminal waiting for the bus to the border. A bus has arrived from the opposite direction, and the returnees on it from Afghanistan, Pakistan, India, Nepal and beyond are like transformed people. How bizarre they look in their newly-adopted native dress, wild hair, and stoned eyes! What a world I must be going to!

My cab driver to the bus station seemed chagrined that I handed him the 10 reals that the trip cost, instead of being a dumb foreigner and asking how much, as I did on arriving, which allows them to charge anything. But in Mashad men often didn't want to take any money at all, because they looked on me as a guest. It happened twice yesterday, first at a teashop in the morning where I had breakfast, and again at the park Hossein's brother drove us to, where the parking attendant refused my money when I offered to pay.

We've been going for two hours. This old road is terrible and the bus is bumping over stones. It's dusty and my seat is in the back of the bus near the engine and the fumes. Also in the bus are two Swiss boys just ahead of me and a party of English and Australians up front. I'm glad I'm alone. I notice foreigners traveling in pairs don't talk to anyone else. Sitting next to me is a Pakistani who told me Christians are considered dirty by Muslims. I wanted to say, "I'm not Christian, I'm Jewish," but felt that might be worse. I also kept silent about the smelly little boy who is squeezed onto the back seat behind me—children don't count here.

We're passing ruined forts and villages in the desert, crumbling fortress walls, broken-in domes, whirlwinds. The roofs of the mud houses of one village are domed, and in the next village flat. Odd, that some villagers are dome-makers and others make flat roofs. The domes seem to be made of mud, which seems quite an engineering feat. My neighbor explained that they build the walls first and then fill the room up with straw and mound the mud on top of the straw until it dries. The men in the villages are wearing beautiful, white chiffon turbans, which are wound around with one long streamer down their backs. But it would be too flashy if I wore one of those, I think.

When we reached the Iranian border where the passports were to be stamped for exit from Iran, no one knew what was going on. One question that I've never been able to get anyone to understand since leaving Europe is How long? How long do we stay here? How long is the trip? Perhaps I'm not expressing myself right, but even the locals who speak English don't understand. They just answer Yes to everything. Is time different to them?

We idled all day at the border—we got there at 11:30 a.m. and didn't leave until 5 p.m. Apparently it was all the Pakistani passports which held us up. I was able to buy bread, cucumbers, green grapes, and tea.

Now, 3 kms. beyond passport control, this is still Iran and we're held up again for another passport check or more mysterious reasons. The road is just terrible, but at least it goes straight across this desert plain, somewhat of a no-man's-land. At the Afghani border we will surely have another long delay, because the Pakistanis are bringing a great variety of goods, mostly plasticware, it seems, back to Pakistan. They go on buying expeditions to Tehran. From there we can get a taxi to Herat, the closest city to the border, where we'll spend the night and leave for Kabul in the morning. I'm anxious to register at the American embassy for mail. Then I'll feel free to travel around and maybe find a place to live for the summer.

My companions are now a French girl of about twenty named Silvaine, who has been teaching in Tehran. A girl traveling alone here does not have an easy time so she is sticking close to me. And two boys, one from Mashad and one from Kabul who, oddly, are nephew and uncle.

I'm so dusty and uncomfortable that arriving in Afghanistan will be all the more moving for it being so hard to get there.

JUNE 20. Herat, Afghanistan. The Afghani border formalities yesterday were again endless and exhausting. Then I squeezed into a jeep share-taxi and got to Herat at 11:30 p.m. The jeep dropped me off in a walled courtyard, a caravanserai, and when I asked to go to the hotel which had been recommended to me, I was told it was too far. (Today I went out for a walk and it was around the corner.) I was dubious about staying in the caravanserai—it was like the large courtyard of a ruined castle open to the sky , with low buildings set into the crumbling, mud brick walls. The courtyard was full of vehicles and activity. A terrace that ran the length of one side, reached by a short flight of stone steps, with a row of beds in the open air where people were already sleeping. Behind, adobe bedrooms with shutters opened onto the terrace, and a few of the Pakistanis took a room together—they had bedding rolls with them. I was offered a private room, but it was filthy and airless and I opted to sleep outside. A number of the other passengers also did, and beds were brought out for us onto the terrace. Before I fell asleep, I lay there looking at vast theatrical ruins beyond the walls in the moonlight. I woke in the clear desert dawn with a biblical scene before me—the caravanserai courtyard, and the fortress balustrades looming over us.

Silvaine, who had stayed in a hotel, and I hired a buggy to see the town, a jumble of unpaved, dusty streets of low, squalid shops. When the driver stopped and got off to pee, squatting against a wall Muslim-style, the horse also let go a stream at the same time—horse and driver perfectly attuned.

I dropped Silvaine at her hotel after our two-hour buggy ride for which we were soaked exorbitantly, and took a long walk by myself to a ruined dome in a pine grove just out of town on a hillside. The guidebook described it as a charming park and I had a vision of water gushing from the rocks, like the park in Mashad. But after a miserable hour's hike in the blazing sun I came to a bone-dry woods with nobody there but some poor workers squatting in the dust. They kindly gave me water and a rug to sleep on. But when I lay down, even in the shade it was too hot and the ants crawled over me.

Like in Mashad, I've been hounded by all the kids in the town who want to practice their English on me, desperate to get through their exams.

Our bus left Herat at 5 p.m., the all night trip having been recommended because of the heat of the desert we had to travel across. From the moment I saw that bus, a hard, small vehicle with no springs, I knew I was in for a miserable night. I could tell that it had no more clutch when we started, and of course it was overloaded. The children ride free since they don't need seats, and just squeeze in anywhere. The rest of us were squeezed in three to a seat—iron seats— and I was in the middle. Hopeless that anything could rescue me from my misery, for the whole route was through desert and the air was dehydrated, I kept saying the 23rd Psalm over and over. Hour after hour I kept my eyes shut and focused on the "green pastures" and the "still waters."

At midnight, we stopped for dinner at an open-air teahouse along the highway under a small grove of dusty trees beside a walled-in modern hotel standing all by itself in the desert— dark, empty, and ghostly in the moonlight. Silvaine and I sat together at one of the tables under the trees from which kerosene lamps were hanging and had pots of tea and shared my last oranges.

I asked the waiter what the hotel was doing there improbably in the desert, and he said it was built by the Russians as a winter resort but was shut now. I tried to learn why anyone would want to stay there in the middle of nowhere, but he couldn't understand more than a few words of English and my Farsi was still rudimentary. Then he pointed over the four-foot wall between the hotel and the tea house and said there was a swimming pool. A pool? I asked. With water? Yes, he said. I went to look over the wall on which robed and turbaned men from the bus were sitting in the dark, and sure enough, there was a swimming pool in the moonlight, full of water. Incredulous, I went back and again asked the waiter about it, and he assured me it was fresh water. Parched, I was ready to go in my underwear, but gave it up—I had no towel and the thought of wet and sticky undershorts on the bus sounded uncomfortable. I kept looking at the water, and back at the bus to see if it was about to leave. Then I decided yes, climbed over the wall, and ignoring the men sitting there with their backs to me, took everything off in the darkness and swam bare-ass in the moonlight. The water was spring water, sparkling, pure bliss after the long, hot, filthy bus ride and the dehydrated air.

The men sitting on the wall didn't turn around, I'm sure of it, and no one else joined me. But it created a scandal. Nobody acted like they saw me, but they did. The bus driver made nasty remarks as I got back on, already dried off in the desert air. I understood him perfectly from the tone of his voice, even without recognizing much more than the word "tourist" that he spat out at me. And my immodest behavior also ruined Silvaine's reputation by association, as it turned out.

En route again, refreshed, I realized that a miracle had happened, that I had been praying and praying for. It was the most unlikely thing in the world that we would come across a Russian swimming pool in the remote desert of Afghanistan! Yet when it was the thing I needed most, it happened, though my prayer was answered in an unusual way. I told Silvaine about a Christian Science tract I had once read, called "God's Law of Adjustment," and how skeptical I had been about the part that claims even if you are lost in a shark-filled sea you can be rescued. Or in my case, riding through the desert. It was my introduction to The Mysterious East.

JUNE 21. After last night's miracle in the desert, refreshed after the swim, the rest of the ride on the road to Kabul was transformed. But, at dawn, an hour before Kandahar, the bus broke down—the clutch finally burned out, of course.

The men got out to pray and I was able to observe them through the window at their devotions in the field beside the bus. This includes, first, ritual squatting to pee, which makes it a quite private act, though difficult, it seems to me, in those flowing native clothes; then washing hands, feet, nose, ears, and mouth—here in irrigation ditches—and finally the kneeling and bowing exercises that go with the prayers. It's a whole system of taking care of oneself, physically and spiritually. Each goes off alone. Some of them go over and over the prayer, kneeling, bowing forehead to ground, and standing up with open hands before them. It's strangely beautiful to see a field with solitary men at prayer scattered here and there.

As the sun rose, everyone got out of the bus and crouched in its shadow, waiting for the relief bus—the desert was flat, the highway straight to the horizon. When Silvaine went off by herself across the field, I suppose to find a ditch to pee in, the men started making jokes about my association with her. They felt free because I had ruined her reputation by my behavior at the swimming pool, and I felt guilty. Squatting in the bus's shadow, a fleshy man, a Pakistani with a pock-marked face, kept leaning toward me and, breathing heavily, asked over and over how many times I had done it with her. We both got very excited as he kept repeating "How many times?" and nudging me, his eyes shining. It was as though his sensual lips were brushing my face and our bodies swayed towards each other. He would point to her, and ask "How many times?" and laugh and poke me lightly with his finger, keeping the sexual tension going. I began to see that pockmarks are not necessarily unattractive.

A rescue bus came, the baggage was transferred to its roof, and we were off again. We stopped in Kandahar, all dust and ruins, and Silvaine kept saying this was a very interesting place, referring to its history as capitol of one empire or another, but I couldn't see anything of interest. Not a tree, just unpaved streets and hovels. A peddler sold me a brown lump of hashish.

Now, en route to Kabul, even with camel herds and the whole ancient scene of the desert, I can't bear it. The heat and dust are more than I can stand. I only dream of the wet Normandy seacoast. Why did I ever come here?

We stop frequently for roadblocks—there seems to be a lot of highway control by the government—or for prayers. In one of the tiny villages we passed I saw a man, stark naked, sitting under a tree nearby with his cock and balls exposed in public, idly touching them. With his overgrown hair and beard I first thought he was the town loony, but he had to be a holy man, a dervish. When he saw me gaping, he let out a yell and what sounded like a stream of curses. What nerve he had to sit there like that! And strange that it was accepted behavior. I wish I'd had more presence of mind and leaned out and talked to him.

Kabul. We arrived at dusk, with the city enveloped in a cloud of dust and nothing to be seen. The whole trip, and the arrival in such a mystifying place, was made more difficult by Silvaine tagging along and being so dependent on me. But night was falling, and she was rightly terrified of being left alone on the streets after dark. It would be assumed that she didn't belong to anyone, and any man would have the right to seize her. She begged me to help her find Les Petites Soeurs de Charité, a French order of nuns with whom she was supposed to stay. I walked around with her in the dusk, trying to find the French embassy where a friend of hers worked who would help her find the Sisters. We finally had to ring the doorbell of the Czech Embassy, and disturbed the ambassador at dinner. But he saw that we were lost and helpless, and generously drove us in his car to the French Embassy. The French ambassador was also having dinner, but he too understood Silvaine's predicament and contacted Silvaine's friend, Mme. Pelleport, who picked Silvaine up in her car. She invited me to lunch tomorrow which I accepted, unlike the usual me who is always turning down invitations.

The Park Hotel (which was the first hotel I came across) is by no means the first-class hotel it claims to be, though it's newly opened and my room is comfortable enough. I'm paying 250 Afghanis, about $3.30, with a private toilet and shower. But it feels not quite finished—it lacks a reading lamp and closet, and there are no hangers of any kind. The most awful ghosts of dead mosquitoes cling to the walls, or they could be a bug that comes to life at night. These pseudo-modern hotels all have picture windows that don't open for air, except for one little screened place.

I'm sitting here smoking the Kandahar hashish, which you are supposed to do here, I guess. I seem to have bites all around my thighs. Fleas in the bus? I hope I haven't brought them here. Or are they already in this room?

I went out and ate a big bowl of yoghurt. Silvaine's guidebook said there is no drinking water in Afghanistan unless it is boiled, but I've been drinking it everywhere. I discovered today that some of that cool, delicious water I had been drinking in a teahouse we stopped at was scooped up by the waiter from the irrigation canal out back. I may have some awful disease incubating in me. But I'm not having diarrhea yet.

Kabul has me stunned—it makes no sense that I can see. It is a huge small village going in every direction, and dusty from the wind—the whole valley was in a cloud of dust this evening. Suddenly I'm here and I don't know where I am. I long to go back to the Caspian, the Black Sea. How can I stay here? My mind is already starting to think of continuing onward— Pakistan, India, Nepal, Burma, Japan—around the world. It's a big letdown finally to get as far as you're going.

I hope I don't have fleas. Could it be this hotel? But I was bitten already when I came in, wasn't I?

JUNE 22. I'm feeling better about Kabul. I went down to the American Embassy and registered for mail. It's on the boulevard to the airport, and nearby on the bare plain is a huge walled compound that is almost a town to itself, with ranch houses, schools, and everything. American families need to feel at home and not as if they were in a foreign land. All their food is imported. The Russians are across town in their own compound. I heard that they have 80,000 troops stationed there.

The city bus out to the embassy was packed, but it only cost 1 Afs.—a cent and a half. The people are very dark and sullen looking, but warm up easily and are kind. They seem overdressed for the heat in loose shirts to the knees, with an old man's jacket or vest over that, baggy cotton drawers, and turbans wrapped around a skull cap with one end hanging down at the rear. I must confess I felt fleas jumping from them to me.

Afterwards, I went to look up some people, friends of a friend, in the Peace Corps who live in a newer section of town, Shari-nau, with many embassies and gardens—a really very pleasant quarter—but they were away. I ate watermelon and a hardboiled egg from street vendors. One man on the street offered me 80 Afghanis for the dollar, so perhaps I can do even better than that. In shops I looked at silk scarves which cost 300 Afs. Does that mean I could get them for 150? And so many beautiful things—plates made of agate, fur coats, brass trays, samovars. I must go to the main bazaar and see what things cost there. After all, this is a neighborhood where foreigners live, so prices must be inflated. It makes me cheerful to think of buying some of these things as presents. And clothing for myself—comfortable sandals, a hat for the sun. Maybe one of those blue cotton outfits that look so comfortable on the Afghans—like baggy pajamas, but close at the ankles, wrist and throat.

I passed a hippie hotel with an inner courtyard café full of shaggy heads and bare feet. They all looked stoned. But drugs seem to be everywhere—that's what a lot of the hippies come here for.

I haven't yet tuned in to the people. Eyes don't melt into yours as you pass, like in Iran. But I was invited into an embroidery shop for tea near Shari-nau Park, not far from the Peace Corps family, by a man who had a Chinese-looking boy—Mongolian?—working for him there. When I asked if it was his son, he said no, he was a friend and winked at me. Later, when he repeated it, I asked, "A special friend?" and he said Yes. He also gave me a piece of hashish to try. Naturally, he deals in everything

My head is spinning. I've got to take it easy in this dry heat. And the dust. And the altitude. How long has it been since I got my cholera shot in Tehran? It takes ten days to get immunity. It's nine days now. My arm, where I got the shot, is quite swollen. I hope it works. I'm praying to keep healthy.

I had lunch at Mme. Pelleport's with Silvaine and two of the nuns she's staying with. Les Petites Soeurs are a new kind of nun who just go and live with the people. They do their own work and live without supervision. Here in Kabul, three live together, two of them keeping house and the other working in a hospital. They make no attempt at converting anyone, just sharing their lives.

Mme. Pelleport spoke about the danger of eating Afghani food. At the beginning people have good resistance to the germs from our healthy diet in the West, but then you become more susceptible. But what can I do? I have to risk it.

Lunch was very French, with a salade de tomates et concombres, stewed slices of meat like pot roast with green beans, a strawberry tart, French cheese, and fruits—washed in some chemical, she said. The cheese and other French food are imported by a cooperative of foreign residents. The Intercontinental Hotel on the edge of town imports everything, she said, including water, to protect the foreigners.

Silvaine is full of plans to tour Afghanistan the next ten days. She wants to go to difficult places like Nuristan where you have to go on horseback. I'm not up to any more traveling for awhile, except maybe to Paghman, a cool, green village I've heard about that's the resort for Kabul in the nearby mountains. I dread getting on the buses here—everything is so hectic, hot, crowded. The trip to the embassy and back this morning seems horrible. After searching for the Peace Corps family I took a cab back to the hotel.

I've got a series of new flea bites down one leg.

JUNE 24. I was out of the hotel at 6:30 a.m. This town wakes up early. I haven't been out at night yet to see how late it stays up. I went for breakfast to the Khyber Restaurant near the grand, colonial-style Hotel Kabul. I was so sick yesterday with stomach cramps that I thought I ought to try this more-or-less western-style cafeteria/restaurant where most tourists go because the food is reputed to be safe. In front of the Khyber terrasse are usually parked a collection of jeeps, land rovers, and campers from Europe, often with inscriptions like "Paris-Kabul Expedition" or "London-Katmandu Or Bust" painted on the side. Driving overland from Europe to this part of the world is still considered in the adventure category. The Khyber is expensive compared to my little native places which cost pennies. I thought at first it was only patronized by hippie types, but then three Afghan officers came in for breakfast.

I went to the government tourist office and spoke to the director, telling him I was here to write a book about Afghanistan and asked him to give me a letter of introduction I could use on my travels around the country. He seemed dubious about my credentials, but nevertheless had his secretary type out an official-looking document, asking anyone to give me every courtesy and consideration. I wonder if it will work?

Afterwards, I took a long walk to the village of Chelsetun on the edge of Kabul, stopping in at several tea houses for refreshment on the way. Two of them refused to take any money. As I walked through the countryside talking to everybody, greeting them with my rudimentary Farsi, people were very gracious, with such courteous manners, touching the heart to express heartfelt greetings or thanks or goodbye. In one tea house I met a writer who said he has finished a book about Afghanistan, to be called "New Afghanistan," which is going to be published by Afghantour, the ministry that promotes tourism. He goes to Paghman too, and perhaps I will see him there.

I had rubber soles and heels put on my sandals in a little village shoemaker's shop that I passed. He charged me about a quarter and did a splendid job of cutting pieces from an old rubber tire and nailing them on. On the way home the strap broke and another shoemaker sewed it together and refused to take any money. With the rubber soles and heels, the sandals are much more practical for the roads, bumpy and rocky as they are, and somewhat softer on the pavement. But oddly, now I have a rubbed place on the instep.

Chelsetun is clustered on a hillside and the houses are built over the streets which follow the contours of the hill. I was tired, the sun was high, and when a young man invited me to his house, I accepted. He led me through more tunnels and alleys than I could imagine a little village like this having. His house was at least two stories high, and the sitting room was on the top floor with windows on both sides, giving air as well as valley views. The floor was covered with a brightly colored rug of geometric design, and on three sides along the wall were thin mattresses and big cushions to lean against. Colorful wall hangings and photographs made the room restful and delightful. Shoes were left at the door, and I was taken into a back room where the host poured water for me to wash, saying I was his guest and the house was mine, like in an old legend.

My host's cousin joined us. Both were students, one studying hotel management and about to start practice-work this summer in a fancy restaurant, and the other aiming for the university. Their English was minimal but we managed. Lunch was on the floor, of course. It was brought in by the boys—no women were in sight. Three loaves of bread wrapped in a cloth, one for each of us. It seemed odd to me that we each had our own loaf, rough slabs called *nan*. Then a tray with a communal omelet, a bowl of yoghurt, and a bowl of apricots. We ate native-style without utensils, using a piece of bread as a spoon. Each of our loaves, I noticed, was only partly eaten.

Then they walked me to the bus where the charming driver and his handsome assistant showed off for me, the foreigner, by acting crazy. I had a seat by the window because Chelsetun is the end of the line. There was a rope up toward the front, dividing the men's section from the women's. The women only had the first row of seats and a standing area behind the driver. The men had the rest of the bus. More people were packed in than I could have believed—no wonder the buses are breaking down all over the highway. After our bus to Kabul broke down, even the bus they dispatched to rescue us was overloaded and it too had a weak clutch. But luckily, by then we were no longer way out in the middle of the desert.

I just bought a small, sweet, expensive mango. They come from Pakistan. When I say expensive, I mean 2 Afs.—3 cents. I'm starting to value the Afghani. My hotel seems expensive now. But a coke at 15 Afs. seems worth it in this dry climate.

New York seems a million miles away, and I can't believe it is possible to get mail here. Today I thought of the village of Asilah outside of Tangier on the Atlantic, how nice Morocco is. I guess I'll be perpetually thirsty here.

JUNE 28. The Karga Dam outside Kabul is so new there hasn't been enough time for vegetation to grow up around the reservoir, and it's bleak. The sun was boiling, though the lake was some consolation and I went swimming. But the bare landscape is too harsh on the eyes. On Fridays, the Muslim day off, at least it's crowded. Everyone at the campground nearby was pretty much a hippie, although there seemed to be a lot of Australians traveling to England or back home. They can drive most of the way. They suggested Kashmir as the place to go for the summer. They say it's like Switzerland. I really don't belong with all these wanderers. Everyone is passing through.

Some Americans I met while swimming suggested coming with them to Paghman. One of them, a man who seems to have always bummed around, had a VW camper. The other two were Los Angeles boys with long hair and beards and pajama pants for clothes and nothing else. At Paghman we lay on the grass under trees by a brook and turned on. People passing by looked at us curiously. It made me feel uncomfortable to behave like that in public, but the others seemed oblivious. One of the hippie boys was saying that the only unhung-up people were the Tibetans and he'd like to live with the Tibetan refugees in north India. The other boy, a stoned-freak type, kept going into fantasies that amused him greatly. "I'm thinking of Afghani feet. Oh man!" Giggle. "Hey, man, how about Afghani garbage? Wow!" I could see that it was a land of legend to him here, and the people of another reality, like Munchkins.

What a wall we put up against the Afghans.

While stoned, I was thinking again that I don't really like drugs. They befuddle the mind. It's like being hit over the head.

Later, at dinner at the Khyber, some English from the lake were there and another boy I met this morning. I keep running into the same people—everybody moving, passing through. I'm living in a transient world.

When I went outside this morning, I saw the city as if for the first time. The mountains around were huge-looking. Usually they are vague from the dust that fills the valley, so you don't really see them. On this clear day it was a quite dramatic landscape. Several people I've spoken to refer to this place as Middle Earth. I've begun to see how handsome the men are.

There was a to-do in the hotel tonight. The police came to arrest an Italian couple who were taking back to Italy 70 kilos of hashish. The stuff had already been packed and cleared for shipment. They were all ready to leave when it was discovered.

I've paid my hotel bill, since I'm leaving in the morning for the Bamian Valley, famous for giant Buddhas carved into the rocks. I booked my bus seat at the government bus company in the bazaar. I have to wake up at 2 a.m. to catch it at 3, and it's a 12-hour trip. It will be horrible— how can we make it in that old wreck of a bus? I know how overcrowded it will be.

JUNE 30. Bamian Valley. The bus trip of 150 kms. took 13 hours over incredibly bumpy and dangerous roads. They were just stones.

On the bus I teamed up with an English girl from Birmingham named Lily and an Italian boy, both part of the wandering tribe. They seem to get a little money from home, pick up a little more by selling dope, mooch when they can, and live in the simplest way. They take all kinds of drugs and are so cool, they make me feel old-fashioned. They have loads of problems, but their style overrides it all.

They've been living in a hippie hotel, the Najib, with a pleasant garden with tables under the trees full of the shaggy and the minimally dressed—all quite friendly with each other, for they keep running into each other all over Asia and Europe in their regular haunts. The language of these world travelers is universally English.

They did me a big favor by advising me to sit on the roof of the bus with them among the piled-up baggage. It was far better than the packed interior with hard seats and no springs. We could see everything and were fairly comfortable sitting on the bedding rolls that most people travel with. When the sun got glaring I pulled my shirt over my head.

The Italian boy had taken some speed and talked half-incoherently for an hour or two, then lapsed into silence for the rest of the trip. I gathered that he's the greatly cherished older son of a painter/sculptor father who is quite successful.

The scenery was spectacular. We followed river beds mostly and the road went through narrow gorges and fertile valleys, although the hills above remained rocky and barren. It was a remote world, similar in appearance to the farming areas I passed on the Turkish-Iranian border or along the Iranian-Russian border on the road to Mashad. But so far nothing has been more exotic than Morocco.

There were a few Afghani men with us on the roof of the bus who took great interest in Lily, who was wearing only flimsy pajamas. Oblivious, she went on rolling joints and smoking them, and at our rest stops, she went off into the bushes where I think she took harder drugs too, for she talked of her "pain killers" and I noticed in her handbag a package of hypodermic needles. The trip continued to be bumpy and the road barely clung to the rocks.

Being with the hippie couple, I again didn't talk much with the Afghani passengers. I felt cut off by being with them. I keep noticing how remote the hippie world travelers are from the local populations. They make no attempt to learn any of the languages.

We passed a family, all of them working by their house in a field, washing things in a stream, and one little girl patting cakes of cowshit, like making mud pies. The method of irrigation in these valleys is simple and seemingly ancient. A stone channel is built to divert water from the river into the fields on either side, or through a house compound for kitchen use or gardening, before returning to the river lower down. These channels are built up like little Roman aqueducts. A river is "milked" by numbers of these channels all along.

People shit everywhere, especially by streams in order to be able to wash themselves, but in the dry air excrement dries fast and becomes the dust that blows in your eyes and mouth. It's probably antiseptic.

When we got to Bamian, Lily led us to the hotel in the village, the Guest House, full of hippies, knapsacks, sleeping bags piled in rooms and corridors. Lily had her own sleeping bag and announced she was sleeping on the floor, which was a wise decision when I saw the beds. There were no private rooms available, and I was shown a bed in a room with two curly-headed young men. But although they greeted me and urged me to stay, I couldn't bear the public living arrangements and fled up the hill to the only other hotel, the government hotel, which is more expensive, but had a room for me. Here too, my bed sags, and there's no hot water at this hour either. It's really a dump. When I was openly critical of the rooms I was shown, this was met with a certain incredulity, perhaps because I look unconventional and was so messy from the trip.

Now, the wind is whistling around my window—the hotel is on a height facing the spectacular carved Buddhas and caves across the valley. It looks like a long walk there.

There are two Swiss boys in sleeping bags on air mattresses beside their VW microbus below in the parking lot. How I envy them.

JULY 1. At dawn in this beautiful valley it's hard to be depressed. It's a little like the Grand Canyon with eroded bluffs in many colors, a snow-streaked mountain range in the distance. If the hills are all bare, the valley floor is lush green and the sound of the rushing river dominates. The houses in the fields are mud brick and designed like little or big fortresses, many with four turrets, one in each corner. On the various hills and peaks around are ruins of cities, palaces, villages. And of course across from the hotel terrace where I'm standing, the famous giant Buddhas surrounded by innumerable dark caves of hermits. The hermits are all gone for a thousand years, they say.

One strange thing about the locals—when I ask "What kind of juice?" or "How many miles?" or "How long?" They always answer, Yes, no matter how you put it.

I had a big breakfast—even drank a can of imported orange juice that cost the fantastic price, for here, of 50 cents—but am thirsty again. I wish I had a gallon of lemonade with ice. The eggs were a mistake, because they make you hot inside. Yoghurt is much better.

An American I met in the ethnographic museum photographing Nuristani sculpture came into the dining room with his wife. They rented a car and driver to come here. The car is a Volga, made in the Soviet Union, slightly old-fashioned looking, but the chauffeur said the car was solidly built, the best car for these roads.

Later. After breakfast I went down to the bazaar and, passing the gate to the path up to the giant Buddha, the keeper, a sweet old man, insisted I take the key and go up to the Buddha's head, so that though I hadn't planned to go this morning I had to, especially since he wouldn't take any money.

Now I'm climbing the hill to the head of the great Buddha, sitting down to rest in the shade of some caves with smoke-blackened roofs. The steps are cut into the rock through tunnels alongside the Buddha. I've been climbing and climbing but can't seem to find this Buddha's head. I've been a little afraid of fainting and falling down the cliff face. I'm even sweating for the first time in a month, for in this dry air you don't sweat, or it dries immediately.

Climbing up, I've reached the head at last, and am in a kind of gallery excavated behind it. Frescoes are painted on the Buddha's head, only fragments now remaining and horribly patched in white plaster, which show the seated Buddha doing various movements with his hands. The rock is cut in a smooth arc over the Buddha's head, framing a postcard view of the valley. Far below is the village street with the Guest House that is painted a clean yellow ochre, but is a pig pen inside.

My first reaction is terror at being so high with no railing to keep me from falling. It's like nightmares, where even with the possibility of going over the cliff, you start being dragged over by some irresistible force.

"AMERICAN FALLS TO DEATH FROM BUDDHA. Notebook is found detailing despondency and depression."

It's really too uncomfortable to stay up here.

Evening. I walked across the valley to where the river runs through a woods, washed my handkerchief and underwear, draping them over bushes to dry, and then got into the water, lay down on the stones and let it wash over me for a long time. It was delicious. I also ate some cherries and apricots that I washed in the river, and don't know if it's from them or the dubious yoghurt I ate in the village, but now I have a touch of diarrhea again.

Heading back to the hotel on paths through cultivated fields, I was stopped on the way by a strange-looking Afghani who invited me to have tea with him. He was clean-shaven, with longer hair than usual, straight black hair falling on either side of his face and wearing a long white gown. He sat me down on a rug and quilt in the shade by an irrigation ditch near his house, and brought tea and bread. But his younger brother who was studying English with a Peace Corps volunteer came over and dominated the conversation, asking me for this and that. He was such a pest I got impatient and left. Oddly, the strange-looking man refused to shake hands with me, although his father who had joined us did. It only occurs to me now, the way he appeared suddenly out of nowhere and wouldn't touch me, that the strange man could have been a dervish. When I asked them about dervishes in the valley, first they said no, there were none, and then said yes, there were many here. But I didn't think to ask him if he was one.

I have now met the Peace Corps worker, a girl named Susan Long, and asked her about living here, but she was discouraging about the possibility of finding a room. She herself has her own room at the hippie Guest House in the village.

I keep being amazed how many streams of water can be drawn off from the river and how widely they can irrigate and finally spill back. It's very sophisticated. Yet they say this valley was destroyed by Genghis Khan. As a religious center, yes, but I wonder if the farming and irrigation ever ceased. Lily, who is still at the Guest House, says it's all owned by lords, and the farmers are tenants or vassals. I saw her this morning on the main street and she talked about going on horseback overland to Pakistan. The boy Lily is going with sold his car in exchange for six horses to make the trip on. They had also wanted to stay on in Bamian for the summer but couldn't find a house.

It's strange to see all the hippies here in this remote valley. It must be one of their stops on the international circuit. The Peace Corps girl recommended Ghazni as a place to live. She said it was one of the cooler places and had interesting bazaars.

I should really resist drinking water when I'm thirsty. It only makes one thirstier to drink. The solution is to adapt to the dryness. You have to accept the thirst.

I've got a small stabbing pain in my left heel and wonder if a worm got in and is eating its way into my body. They say you get worms from going barefoot where animals have shit, and there was horseshit by the river.

I walked up to the lesser Buddha and looked into some of the caves around it. Far off, I saw a carpet spread in front of a cave and went to investigate, having been told that there were still hermits in some of the further caves. But it seemed to be a family living there, and the women were in great consternation over my passing—they covered their faces and turned to the wall. When I crossed a field to go back to the road, a woman coming toward me stopped in alarm, covering up, so I took another path and bypassed her. When the women are covered up in the total veil called the *chadri* and carrying a bundle on their heads, they look picturesque, like in the National Geographic. They wear pants underneath of flowered material, very loose, bunched at the waist and gathered at the ankle. The men's costumes are also handsome here, with long striped coats lined in a cotton print, and sleeves decoratively over-long, which they hardly ever put their arms through, but wear them cape-like over their shoulders. The turbans wound over an embroidered or crocheted skullcap give them a wild look.

When I got back, the hotel manager warned me that it isn't safe to walk alone through the fields as I did today, because there are leopards in this valley.

I went to the post office to mail some letters and found the postmaster/telephone operator sitting like a lord on carpets, surrounded by local friends who looked on admiringly while he talked on the telephone. He was a dapper man, though his friends were country people and quite grubby—one of them from Mazar-i-Sharif was almost black. He said it was hot there and I believe him. The postmaster invited me to sit down next to him, before telling me that it was too late to mail the letters today. He was wearing striped pajamas and holding his prick—so the men do touch themselves in this country, but I still get very little sensual feeling from them. Another thing, I talk and talk with them but never feel I've made a friend. Is sexuality out because of my age? In Iran I certainly didn't feel any such thing. Here, I'm not sure where the sexuality is.

It's amusing how people wear their pajama-type clothes under modern business suits and uniforms, and can take off their suits anywhere and be native again.

JULY 2. Last night at dinner a German couple, the Holzmanns, who are actors in the Schiller Theater of Berlin and spend their annual vacation traveling around the world, said southern India was the most fabulous place they've ever been, with colorful religious processions and decked-out sacred cows. They had just gone to Band-i-ameer, the lakes, and would gladly have taken me in their car if they had known I wanted to go. They're living in one of the yurts behind the hotel—a Mongolian tent covered in felt—and asked me in for drinks. It was much more luxurious than my room. They're flying to Peshawar next, but are dreaming of the South Pacific where they'll feel free to eat the fruit. Here, they don't dare eat either salad or fruit, so I ate their apricots.

The electricity is on only from 7 p.m. until 10 p.m.—you can hear the generator behind the hotel when it's working. At a quarter to ten the lights flickered in warning, and I hurried back to my room just in time. One nice thing in Afghani hotel rooms, the rugs are thick and beautiful. So I moved the mattress onto the floor, which was much more comfortable.

This morning, an American family whom I met at breakfast gave me a lift in their rented taxi to the lakes at Band-i-ameer. The 75 kilometers to the lakes took us four hours, on the meanest road ever, through desert hills like in cowboy movies, covered with clumps of bristly plants. We saw horsemen with rifles and bandoleers of shells across their chests. Protection against wolves perhaps, or bears, or Kuchee nomads? But the car, an Opel, had a hard time on the steep, rocky road. Everyone says you need one of those sturdy Russian Volgas or a Mercedes for these roads. The driver was quite embarrassed by his car's performance. It won't last long here. Near a Kuchee nomad camp with huge tents and grazing camels and horses, we had to get out to help push the car up a hill. Another time, a group of men with donkeys loaded with brush helped push us up another one. They had a strange-looking dog with cut off ears and tail—I thought to keep them from freezing in the winter, but the chauffeur said they're bred for fighting and that way other dogs couldn't seize them by their ears or tail. A huge, vicious dog chased the car for awhile.

…We have arrived, impossibly, at this impossible lake in the air, like a bathtub, its unusual sidewalls either built up by some strange limestone action or the erosion of the ground around it. It stands there in a dry, rocky valley with no vegetation. An informal campsite has grown up on one side of the lake with campers' tents and Land Rovers. On the other side is an inn next to a *madrasa*, a religious school. Whatever the guidebook says, I feel the lake has been created over the ages, first by men damming a stream or spring, and gradually building up the sides. Then nature took over and minerals in the water coated the man-made walls. So the lake looks like a great stone tub, brim full and spilling in waterfalls here and there. The water is so clear you can see schools of fish. Around the edge grow mint and other herbs, making the whole place smell sweet.

We walked around the rim to where the school and inn are, which was scary, for the sides drop down a long way and the stone is often wet and slippery. We swam off a ledge with a large crowd of Afghans as audience. They don't swim, though they often bathe in streams. But each goes off by himself, for it has a certain ritual quality to it—bathing is part of the religion. How clear and blue the water was, but so cold, it was hard to stay in for long.

The charming manager of the hotel is here, having driven in a jeep with some elegant foreign ladies. I asked him about dervishes in Bamian and he said the religious people who are always praying are called *sufis*, but there is no *khanega* (dervish house). In Kabul, there are *khanegas*. He said to ask.

Before we left, I went into the *madrasa*, which seemed to be the remnant of a ruined mosque or shrine, and upstairs in a tiny room found the mullah. He was a beautiful young man who had six months to spend here, teaching, before being transferred to Kandahar. He teaches three classes, a total of 75 students, from the nearby village.

It seemed a shame to make such a difficult journey for only a few hours at the lake. It's a place to spend days in. Driving home, we had to continue pushing the car up the worst hills.

The dining room was full of Americans tonight. I ate with the German couple. Holzmann looks a lot like Merce Cunningham, tall and elegant with a handsome, ravaged face. With the Schiller Theater he and his wife go to all the cities of Germany and have even played Lincoln Center in New York. The couple recently went to Russia to promote a film he was in about the Sorge spy ring. They say the bread in Russia is the best in the world. But the bread here called *nan* is very good too, made of whole wheat grown in the desert. The daughter in the car today told me about a Peace Corps worker who went on a diet of nan and tea. At first he lost a lot of weight, but later gained it back. I'm sure that the local nan is almost a complete food.

I overheard an Afghan guest telling a tableful of Americans that people here have twice as much freedom as in Iran or Pakistan. Tell that to the women.

For the second time I've gone out to ask for a candle for the night. The manager said he had told the hall boy to get me one. Later, a boy knocked, bringing me a kerosene lantern that smelled bad. But the lights didn't go out at 10 as usual. Perhaps this being the Sabbath eve, they're left on longer.

JULY 3. At breakfast, I spoke to a middle-aged woman who is with the Peace Corps and here in Bamian for a week on what she calls an indoctrination trip. She's about 55 and from New York where she worked as a secretary. Now she's teaching secretarial skills to Afghans in Kabul. They'll only learn to type English.

On their way back to Kabul the Holzmanns dropped me off at the Red City, a ruined fortification on a peak 20 miles from the hotel. I've climbed to the top and am perched on a ledge looking over the valley and the tortured rocks of the opposite range—they look rich in mineral deposits, like Montana. I've got to climb down again but am somewhat afraid—going up is one thing, coming down another.

I'm sure this hill of ruins is full of treasures. Even the stones look exciting, for they are in all colors and many look like alabaster or agate, perhaps some lapis lazuli. So little has been excavated. Perhaps there are corridors through the rocks, and rooms too, but it's all buried. The only other people around are a party of French students, who have just started down -- as usual, both boys and girls were wearing the briefest of shorts. I tried to speak to them but they are so self-contained they're hardly interested in anyone else. Some local men came up the hill with guns and I asked what they were after. I think they said birds. The hillside was littered with porcupine quills, though.

After climbing down, I took another cold bath in the stream below, then walked to the road and started for home. Clouds appeared, an astonishing and delicious sight in this land. A truck finally came by and picked me up for 10 Afs. I got up into the back among a group of evil-looking men, one of whom greedily poked my shoulder bag inquisitively.

When I got back to the village, two young men invited me in for tea. They're police officers, and are billeted in a room together in the long row of cubbyholes along the main street, most of them used for businesses but obviously some as living quarters. Their room had a big double bed, and rugs on the floor where we sat. There was also a kitchen in back, with a young boy servant from Wakhan (near Pamir) whose cot was in there. I stayed for a pleasant half hour, but nothing was lit between us. They are married with children, but their families aren't with them.

I feel quite frustrated with Afghan men. There's not much warmth from them, and I get mostly politeness. I don't even see much warmth between them, in spite of that double bed they share. There's very little sexual stimulation here, even though the men are handsome. But I'm still very much an outsider and know hardly anything about this part of the world.

I saw the English girl, Lily, and an American boy on horseback racing down the village street. They looked so happy. I guess they are practicing up for the ride to Pakistan.

I went to the river and bathed again—just lying there comfortably on the pebbles while the water washed over. The Holzmanns said in Africa you can't swim in lakes or rivers because of the danger of bilharzia, an organism that gets into your body and eats up your liver. I hope they don't have that here.

Back at the hotel, I met two Brazilian boys with their young mother. They have come from Thailand where the father works in lumber, and are on their way back to Brazil. But the plane to Kabul has been canceled, so they can't get back in time for their flight out tomorrow. The clouds I saw may have been the reason for the cancellation. The alternative to going back on the plane is to charter a bus that costs $80 and holds about 10 people. But the Brazilians can't find that many people to go back to Kabul tonight. The Americans who took me to Band-i-Amir flew back to Kabul that evening. But the plane out of here is always chancy.

I've heard a lot of scary things about the complications of leaving Afghanistan. You need an exit visa, and if returning, a re-entry visa—a long process. And I've heard more discouraging things about the problem of sending things out of the country, like the rugs I want to buy. You have to go to customs and spread *baksheesh*, then to the tourist office, and then to the post office or the shipping company. It's a long and involved process, and not only are they difficult about proper packing, but a lot of the stuff gets confiscated or never arrives.

Before dinner at the hotel, incredibly, it rained a little and got chilly. I stood out on the terrace watching the valley as the sun went down, the extraordinary landscape presided over by the Buddhas carved into the hillside. Such beauty and peace. And four Petites Soeurs in their black and white habits going down the path from the hotel to town.

After dinner the Brazilian family, who were unable to leave, came to my room and we talked until lights out. The Brazilian boys are going to school in the U.S., one to Swarthmore, and the other to Lehigh University for graduate work in engineering—science and technology is what Brazil needs. The older boy kept touching his cock while talking, a Latin mannerism, but odd to see here, and especially in front of his mother. They were all quite hurt that some children threw stones at them today. But it's quite possible the children were guarding women doing laundry or something. They raved about Katmandu. They agreed with me about the hashish being no good here, but they said the

Nepalese hash was wonderful—everything is anti-climax after Nepal. I'd like to go, but it's another couple of thousand miles. Besides, I came here.

This is my true nature coming out, to be friendly to a lot of people.

JULY 4. I'm at the post office, mailing letters and postcards. I was asked to sit down again with the postmaster, my postcards were taken into another room, and I'm still waiting. It's not like any post office I've ever seen, although there is a scale visible. I'm not sure what the procedure is and have a feeling it's going to take some time. The letters are on aerogramme forms, so there should be no problem with them since the stamps are already printed on. I suspect I'm in the wrong room—but perhaps not, and things are done this way here.

The postcards have been brought back stamped by the assistant, who then went to fetch a rubber stamp to cancel them, after which he disappeared with a triumphant smile. It took ten minutes to get the letters mailed. At breakfast, a guest, an ex-governor of Kabul province, said that if you come to Afghanistan you must accept inefficiency as an element of the culture and should keep your sense of humor.

As I was walking down the hill from the hotel, a jeep stopped with an American, a Japanese, and an Afghan inviting me to go with them to Band-i-Ameer. But I remembered that long, bumpy ride, and besides, I didn't have my bathing suit with me.

I've climbed a hill of ruins in the center of the valley, a town destroyed by Genghis Khan eight hundred years ago. I've been poking around the ruins. In the sudden destruction there must have been tons of stuff buried, still unexcavated. On my way here some boys offered me old coins. There's another boy sitting near me and I fear he's going to follow me around, trying to extract baksheesh for his company or guidance. Looking over the valley from this hill, it appears as if the ancient towns and villages were basically cave dwellings with an overlay of buildings. That way, the people could live on the hillsides and not take up valuable farmland. Today, the farmers in the fields below seem to be occupied largely with opening and closing irrigation ditches.

The sun is too hot to sit in, even this early, but I'd like to outsit the boy. He speaks English, thanks to the work of Susan Long, the Peace Corps worker. I learned yesterday that she was born and raised in Brazil. The perfect young idealist. I feel what all these Peace Corps kids are doing—teaching them our language, and typing and shorthand, though only in English—is simply indoctrination, getting them on our side.

Susan thought the religious teacher I met at Band-i-ameer must have been posted there as a political punishment—there's a lot of revolutionary ferment or at least dissatisfaction among the young. With the Soviet Union next door, the example of socialism must be seductive. Certainly the women here must know that the position of women over there is a lot better.

When I came down from the hill, a boy approached me from the fields and another boy joined him a little way along. They were obviously up to no good. There was a stupid menace about them, though all they did, finally, was ask for 5 Afs. Luckily there were people along the road, or I'm sure they would have attacked me.

I'm quite nervous about the local people now. There are nice men and not so nice men, as anywhere. But here I feel a positive danger, especially in their curiosity about my shoulder sack. I don't feel safe out walking. The danger of a dog, or children, or scary men like on the truck yesterday—I saw them again today, driving mules loaded with hay, and this time I was glad to see them since I was trying to out-walk my evil boys. It will be interesting to see how my feelings about the Afghans develop.

I notice that donkeys and swans honk almost alike.

I've met a teenage brother and sister from Kabul who are at the hotel with their parents— their father was governor of Kabul province six years ago and is now retired, and their mother [Shirlee Taraki, now President of the Afghanistan Women's Rescue Committee] is American and Jewish. The children, Joseph and Lisa Taraki, study in the United States, the boy at Lake Forest Academy and Lisa at Mills College where she knew Minu Kazemi, a lovely Iranian girl I met when I gave a poetry reading there. Minu was faced with the not-uncommon nightmare of returning to Iran after graduation, when she'd be sold by her family to a rich old man—her college degree would only make her the more desirable, and expensive. Her one hope of escape was to marry a westerner before she had to go back. I felt so sad for her.

Joseph and I discussed the Red City where he went with his family this morning. They also thought the hill must be full of tunnels and rooms. But it's just as well that nobody opens it up now until the present king is gone, he said, because the treasures inside would just be robbed.

The assistant manager of the hotel told me about getting married in his last year of high school. His father announced to him he had picked out a wife for him. He said he wasn't ready to get married yet, but his parents said they were old and wanted to see him married before they died. So he agreed. He said that all young men are gotten wives by their parents in that way. The boy never gets to pick out a girl. I wish I could ask him if he loves his wife.

There are a whole bunch of AID (Agency For International Development) people at the hotel. The men who offered me the lift to Band-i-amir this morning were with AID. The way all the countries have AID missions here in different areas of the economy, it's like the country is divided up among the stronger nations of the world, a system they've worked out to keep it neutral.

The ex-mayor of Kabul and his family went to eat with Susan Long, the Peace Corps volunteer, at the Guest House tonight.

JULY 5. At breakfast, the manager referred to a high political figure as having "fallen off a cliff" and was staying home. Thinking of the rocky landscape of Afghanistan, I asked if he was badly injured, and was told it was a political cliff he fell off.

He also told me about the filming of "Horseman," a movie about Afghanistan based on a novel by James Michener. He was assigned to show the American actress playing the Kuchee heroine around. She wanted to visit the nomad camps and meet Kuchees, so he took her to visit them up here and also down south at their winter camp in the desert near Pakistan. He said the men wear their hair long, "longer than yours," and greased, and toss it about while dancing.

The manager asked me about my family and I told him how we were scattered all over. He said that his family frequently gets together in one room, and in any case they mostly live in the same house. I think he means the men get together. I'm sure it's a source of security and confidence.

This morning in the bazaar while I was getting new soles and heels on my shoes, made out of rubber tires, a man stopped and suddenly spit a big gob of something on my pants leg. Of course I protested and some men nearby joined in with me, as he walked away. Now what made him do that?

Afterwards, I climbed the mountain that the smaller Buddha is carved into, a perilous ascent. Passing by caves, I definitely heard voices and saw a strange, crazy-looking man duck into one of the caves. There must still be a few hermits around.

Coming down, I met the Petites Soeurs from Kabul, who have spent the night at Band-i-amir, but it was obvious they didn't want a man in their female world. I sometimes suffer the fate of all too-friendly people—rebuff.

I again walked by the city ruined by Genghis Khan. It's endlessly interesting to look at. The city was so horribly destroyed and the inhabitants so brutally slaughtered, that it has never been built on since. The hill is taboo.

JULY 7. My last morning in Bamian Valley. Four German doctors who have been camping here by the hotel in the parking lot are going to drive me back to Kabul.

Settling my bill, the manager lowered it from seven days rent to five—*baksheesh*. The hotel, crummy as it is, is practically charging luxury prices for this country. But that way they keep out the hippies who are forced to stay in the Guest House in the bazaar. I also learned that foreigners pay three times the fare on the airplane than the Afghans do. He told me we are at 8000 feet here—that's why it has been so cool, and the growing season is so short. Melons can't grow here.

I'm waiting for my four German doctors to start. They have all graduated medical school at Tubingen and are having a *Wanderjahr*. Their VW bus is packed full of their camping gear and it's amusing to see them getting ready in the parking lot beside it, brushing their teeth, transferring drinking water from a tank to a smaller jug by means of a tube, taking a last panoramic photo of the valley—they are so delightfully busy, I can't even describe all the things they are doing. And how well they cooperate and function together, so calmly and efficiently— so well organized. They're wearing blue-green surgeon's pajamas, which fit in very well with the native clothes, but are snugger. They're utterly charming, and I suddenly feel quite shy about going with them. Now they're checking the motor, and the air pressure in the tires. Two of them are pumping one of the tires up with a hand pump, and two others are putting the water from the open jug into a portable water jug. Now they're letting air out of the tire and pumping it up again—all very mysterious. They've been sleeping by the bus on air mattresses. When they stood around this morning eating breakfast out of plastic plates, I was curious about what it was—it seemed to be wholesome, nutritious and unexciting—but safe—probably packets of expedition food.

Kabul. The trip back took the whole day. We went a different route, more roundabout, than coming, and for the first time Afghanistan seemed beautiful. In fact, one remote valley was so fertile and the town so charming, I thought I could live there. This route finally connected with the main highway to Kabul, a modern road, where we could drive normally, though we were stopped every 20 kms. or so to pay tolls.

En route we came upon a warm mineral spring, enclosed in a cement basin, right by the road. We stripped off our clothes and soaked. There was already a Canadian threesome in the pool who were planning to drive in their camper as far as Japan. Everybody I meet is going on to India and further. It makes me feel stodgy not to be going on.

In the dark, cooled by a rain, Kabul seems quite pleasant. I've checked into the Tourist Hotel in Shari-Nau, where my room with bath is 200 Afs. The hotel has a building on the street, an inner garden and an annex at the back where I am. There's a sign up on a bulletin board in English: No Smoking Hashish in Hotel. Perhaps that's only for the police. The embassy also had a notice posted about drugs, warning that the Afghan police were getting tougher. But in the drain in my bathroom floor are broken hypodermic needles.

I'm going to eat simply from now on—mostly *nan* and tea. I'm convinced there is nothing healthier. But for my first night back, I'm splurging on a Chinese restaurant, the only one in Kabul. The waiter, a student in a university agricultural faculty, has been talking to me about the poverty and corruption of the wealthy, how the wealth goes out of the country and most people remain jobless and poor. He says all the young people know the score about what is going on. It's considered a disgrace for someone like him to work, but he and his friend are working here as waiters anyway. They plan to go to America for awhile when they finish their studies. He denies that the Afghan people smoke hashish—they only sell it to foreigners. Then he admitted maybe five percent, the jobless, smoke to forget their troubles and feel good. He also told me he thinks the tourists are dirty.

JULY 8. I'm in a humble teahouse having tea and *nan*. Eating a melon gave me diarrhea, so I'm back to bread and tea for awhile. It's thundering and we seem to be about to have another storm. These are unusual summer rains for Kabul—people say the monsoons have drifted over from India.

I went by cab to the carpet bazaar. I'm getting smart and taking cabs to save my feet. Now my head is reeling from the beautiful rugs I saw. I'm beginning to believe in flying carpets. I was told that Mazar-i-Sharif is best for new carpets, but for old ones Kabul is best.

Gerd, one of my German doctors, came with me to buy a rug to take back to Germany. He confused things by offering too high a price at the beginning. Inexplicably, the doctors have brought all their old clothes from Germany to sell here in the bazaar. Shirts especially are in demand, they say.

I've become especially fond of Mongolian looks, and on my way out of a carpet shop where an oriental-looking young man, the rug dealer's assistant, was reclining on a pile of carpets, I impulsively hugged him. Everyone in the shop laughed—it was obviously all right to do that. He actually kissed me back when I hugged him. Maybe I am starting to tune into these people. It's so beautiful to stand there, holding hands and looking endlessly into each other's eyes—they don't mind at all. At a fur shop, a man's eyes almost hypnotized me.

While we were looking at old books in a stall, a boy offered to take us to a shop where there was a really old book. The shopkeeper took it off a shelf and unwrapped it for us, and it turned out to have 26 beautiful, old, hand-painted Persian miniatures as illustrations. He wanted $2,000 for it and won't come down.

I bought a *lunghi*, a turban, a seemingly endless length of white cloth and have practiced winding it on. But will I have the nerve to wear it? It would keep the sun off my head, at least.

My stomach doesn't feel good today. Gerd gave me charcoal pills for it.

JULY 10. At the Khyber for breakfast, a strange man who claimed to be a Peruvian diplomat stationed in Delhi joined me at my table. He was wearing a gaudy shirt and was very thin and hopped up. He said he was driving a motorcycle to London, testing it for the manufacturer. Now he was waiting for a telegram from his wife who might be joining him. So we got on his motorcycle and rode to the embassy to see if it had come, but the embassy turned out to be closed today for the Muslim sabbath.

I've been asking likely people on the street about a dervish house, a *khanega*, and one man—I asked him because he had a beard and seemed religious—denied again and again he knew of any. Finally, the third time I asked (like in a fairy tale) he told me where a *khanega* was located, across the river in the oldest part of town on the far side of the bazaar, so I went in search of it. I've been told it's dangerous for foreigners to go there, though I've been many times to the bazaars and tea houses.

By asking in my inadequate Farsi and with the help of a small boy as a guide through the complicated alleys, I found the address, a walled house like any other, and when I knocked, I was taken to the master dervish, an old, kindly, bearded man. His son and a friend were sent for to translate— they're minor government officials or civil servants. I explained through them to the old man that I was interested in Sufism and he told me that every Thursday night, Muslim Sabbath eve, the dervishes gather in his temple, and stay up all night chanting the name of Allah until dawn. So I had just missed the meeting. The old man had been up all the previous night and I had undoubtedly awakened him. His son said he'd take me next Thursday night to the meeting, and also to the Chishti dervishes who make music. The old dervish was part of the Naqshe order, which I had heard about in Gurdjieff's writings, but when I asked about the whirling dervish dancing Gurdjieff taught, he said that tradition, for them, had disappeared some centuries before.

The old man had some small boys, pupils under the charge of a little hunchback mullah, demonstrate the chanting for me—you expel the breath with a loud Hoo!, and on the intake breath you gasp the name of Allah, perhaps to breathe him in, repeating this without pause and in rhythm. Then he made me practice it, while the old man complimented me, exclaiming, "See how he prays!" This chanting alone apparently leads to whatever religious state is sought for. Of course it's also a breathing exercise, though that kind of forced breathing must hurt the throat after awhile.

After tea was served, the son and his friend invited me to visit some holy tombs on the outskirts of this area, the oldest part of Kabul. The government project they work on, the Pactia Development Project is a vast internationally-funded scheme to irrigate and reforest the desolate south. While we walked to the tombs which lay not far off, out beyond the last houses of the city, my friends prepared a joint by half-emptying a cigarette and refilled it with chips of hashish mixed with the tobacco, which we passed between us. These saints in the tombs, they said, were actually leaders of Muslim armies who came to convert the Buddhists of Afghanistan and died in battle, but their tombs looked to me more like Buddhist temples—open wooden structures with overhanging roofs supported by crude poles, with flags and streamers flying from lances on the roof. Inside, the sarcophagi were enclosed by grillwork screens—veiled women were praying to one side, opposite us. We visited several tombs, walking along the stony, barren hillside above a poor section of the city my guides said was a squatters' town, where people had built their houses without government permission. The houses looked substantial, built of the local stone, but the only water was far below them in the valley, so it had to be carried up.

We followed a goat track around the bare hillside that led us through a gap in the mountains surrounding Kabul, which was guarded by an old fortress. This gap was the site of the invasion of Kabul and we passed old cemeteries with flat tombstones like beds, engraved with flowery Arabic script. These were the graves of soldiers fallen in the fierce battles that had taken place here, where the invaders had fought their way through this gap to take the city and convert the population to Islam. On the other side of the mountain through the gap was a lush valley with marshes and herds grazing and irrigated orchards and gardens—the food supply of the city, such as it was.

We kept climbing on the goat trail, far above the city below, the blazing blue sky above us, and my friends pointed out to me a green spot, high up on the stone mountainside we were heading for. When we got there, it turned out to be a cleft in the mountain, sheltering a small, pretty plaza with a few shady trees and beds of flowers and a small temple. On the plaza there were some men, caretakers I thought, engaged in cooking over small fires, making tea. My friends said that the temple was built over a sacred spring in an underground cave. To get to this spring you had to squeeze through a jagged gap in the rock and climb down slippery stone steps. It looked very dark below and the gap in the rock too narrow to squeeze through. My friends urged me, saying that it was quite pleasant down there with a wooden divan to sit on, and that dervishes came there to fast, drink the waters, and pray. But the hashish had brought out my fears and I couldn't make myself wriggle down into the blackness of that hole.

The men on the plaza turned out to be a group of hashish makers, preparing hashish for sale—this was a hashish factory. They were a wild-looking bunch with droopy mustaches in lean, weathered faces, with black turbans and baggy bloomer pants and dark vests, reminding me of the soldiers of Genghis Khan, or Turkish horsemen riding out of the East, the invaders of Kabul. But they invited us to have tea and one even spread his coat for me on the low, surrounding wall to sit on. As we sat drinking tea and munching some unfamiliar sweets they gave us, I was able to observe the preparing of the hashish. It's odd about cannabis. In Morocco they just use the young leaves of the plant for *kif* and throw the rest away. Here they just use the pollen, and in other places the sap.

To make hashish, first a handful of the pollen is pressed between the palms into a hardish lump that is heated over the fire. The lump is heated repeatedly, while being pressed as hard as possible between the palms. No moisture is added, but the natural gum it contains makes it stick together when heated and squeezed. It takes great strength to press the hashish powder into a paste. The worker not only cooks the hashish cake but, as I observed, keeps putting his own hands over the fire to heat them – their hands were like cured leather from years of this. Eventually the hashish ends up as flat cakes, the thinner the better, confirming what I had heard that the wafer-thin kind is considered the best. We were each given a piece of newly-pressed hashish for *baksheesh*.

We next had to try it out. One man filled a water pipe with charcoal, put crumbs of the hashish on top of that, more charcoal, and more bits of hash, then lit the pipe and passed it around. After taking one puff from the long stem of the water pipe, each of the men fell down immediately, rolling on the ground, coughing painfully. I've noticed from the teashops that they always do that and wonder why the water in the water pipe doesn't cool the smoke and make it more bearable—but it's still a fiery draught. One drag is plenty. When my turn came, I didn't inhale much, because what I had already smoked on the way up there had made me nervous. In fact, I was sweating and felt like fainting. My friends saw my distress and told me to go wash my face from an earthenware jug of water. It always makes me nervous to smoke hash with strangers and in a strange place, even though this was a very pleasant spot. We were under trees with a spectacular valley view, and the people were treating us with great courtesy as guests. Unfortunately, I didn't get loving vibrations from them. I kept wanting to make eye contact, but no one responded. Perhaps they didn't completely trust me as an outsider. Perhaps they thought I would betray them to the police.

So when my friends decided to go, I was relieved—or rather, by no one saying he wanted to leave or stay, we found ourselves getting up together, and with many handshakes, left. On the way we stopped by a flower bed to look endlessly at the geraniums—they were brilliant and shimmering shades of red in the clear light. Hashish makes you appreciate flowers. And the warmth of the sun.

But clinging to the narrow path walking away, I was afraid that I would fall down the steep mountainside, that I would start leaning over and be dragged down by the force of gravity. I was also somewhat afraid that once we had left the shrine, the laws of hospitality wouldn't protect us anymore, and the hashish makers would come after me. I was especially afraid of losing my shoulder bag with passport, diary, and travelers' checks, but I always am.

Back at Jadi Maiwand, the main street of the old city, I took a cab home. Now that I know the fare is 20 Afs., I just hand that over to the driver and there are no arguments.

On my way to my room, I stopped into the hotel restaurant and found my German friends with maps and guidebooks in serious conference around a table. They were about to leave for India and we exchanged addresses. It was a very moving parting as I hugged each in turn, for I realized that they too felt sentimental about leaving me. The charcoal pills they have given me turned out to be the best stomach medicine I have found, better than Mexiform, Enterovioform, and all the other prescription drugs that you can buy here without prescription from a drugstore.

But with all the hashish and the strange activities, I feel quite disoriented even now, some hours later.

JULY 11. My new friends from the dervish house came at five after work—a formal visit. I had incense burning, and music on my transistor radio, and served a variety of sticky sweets from the Indian candy shop, a bowl of fruit, drinking water and ice from the hotel kitchen. They didn't touch the eats—naturally, because I'm not a Muslim and it's unclean. But they showed me how to wind on my turban and perhaps I'll wear it tonight when I go to dinner at the Sicelofts, the Peace Corps people.

After they left, I went into the bathroom to put some lotion on my face because it felt leathery from the dryness here, and looking in the mirror started crying—Asia has opened me up. I felt unaccountably afraid and very far away. But I have enough money with me, I'm staying in a comfortable hotel, and I already run into people I know everywhere—Kabul is small enough for that. This afternoon, for instance, going into a restaurant for lunch, I met my German doctors (who left later in the day) who gave me the lift from Bamian. They've been camping outside the city and were bringing their VW bus in to be serviced before leaving. It's a fact of life here that friends and acquaintances are leaving all the time—everyone except me seems to be passing through. It also looks to me like my face is changing, becoming the underneath me. Perhaps I should cut my foolish-looking, long hair--though plenty of Afghanis have long hair, mainly country people. And the wandering young are long-haired of course.

It's a relief to have reached here. And to stay put for awhile. I was on tour on the West Coast all of April. In May I visited my parents in Florida. June spent in traveling overland to Afghanistan, and we're well into July now. But by September I'll be on the long route back.

Tonight at dinner at the Sicelofts the other guests were a group of Peace Corps volunteers. The host, who is an official, said the Peace Corps program is being reconsidered, since the U.S. government feels that perhaps too large a part of it is devoted to teaching English and not enough to helping with real problems. My feelings completely. One of the volunteers said, "But that's what we can do well." Apparently there had been an attempt to use them to help with AID's agricultural program, but AID didn't like them or find them useful. I really don't know how those bright young people, idealists presumably, can justify what they are doing here. What do the villagers need to learn English for anyway?

I found myself blabbing too much about going to the sacred pool in the grotto and the hashish factory. I hope nobody tips off the narcs. But one girl was interested in Gurdjieff and that set me off.

Someone raised the question as to whether the Kuchee nomads were not a form of migrant labor, since they worked for the farmers wherever they went. Someone else said that one of the pleasures of going to Pakistan (besides it being green and humid) was that, because of the British having ruled there, a railroad starts at the border (Afghanistan hasn't got a railroad), and the cities have fine buildings and good civil administrations and real sewers.

The dogs bark, bark all night here. I'd really be afraid to go out on the street for anything this late. It sounds like they're roaming in packs out there, like wolves. Maybe they are wolves.

JULY 13. I've booked a seat on a small, elegant and un-battered Mercedes-Benz bus to Mazar-i-Sharif. I'm almost sorry not to be going on one of the government buses that are so packed with people. Here I'm supposed to have a seat to myself.

When the boy came to my room at five this morning to wake me, self-consciously pushing at his crotch, I was already awake with my usual nerves over missing the bus. The boy asked for my radio and then for my turban. I gave him 10 Afs. and also left a pair of zoris that hurt my feet. That may have consoled him a little. But I feel ashamed of myself for being such a stingy tipper to the hotel help. Then I succeeded in taking the correct city bus out to the edge of the city where this bus was leaving from.

As I feared, my bus is now full of children and they don't have seats on the theory that only adults need seats and you can put any number of children in between. Of course, one puked right beside me as soon as we left.

Out in the country the men are often bearded. Should I too grow a beard?

Squatting to pee, the men do it with a kind of control, as though it must be done (or aimed) very carefully, and indeed with all the drapery they wear they'd better aim well. My Levis don't allow me to pee that way. I feel exposed when I'm standing up against a tree or rock, but squatting makes it a much more private act.

We've gone through the Salang Pass. This road is really amazing the way it cuts through the mountains, over the Hindu Kush. It's very high and, after the heat and dust of Kabul, the air is deliciously cold. There are kilometer posts at regular intervals giving the mileage to the Russian border—for it was the Russians who built this road and the tunnel. Going through the long Salang tunnel, an amazing engineering feat at this altitude, is always a novelty. When we came out of the tunnel, the driver stopped the bus and the men went out to gather some ice to take home—it seems more like packed snow. It felt good to be chilly for a few minutes in the mountain air.

Once over the mountains there are small cedar trees on the mountainsides, yurts here and there, rice fields. From what I see, I believe that my theory that the lakes of Band-i-Ameer were originally man-made is correct, for on the way down from the Salang pass we passed numbers of small artificial lakes and ponds with raised walls on two or three sides, built by the farmers for irrigation. The difference is that at Band-i-Amir the lakes were abandoned and the mineral content of the water coated the walls with stone, hiding the man-made internal structure. And perhaps land erosion around the lakes increased the bathtub effect. They are all essentially dammed-up streams.

The soldiers I see are strangely closed-faced. In Kabul, too, where they patrol the streets, they're unfriendly. They look malnourished and alien to the population.

Suddenly, nearing Mazar, we're with the dome-builders again. Ruins everywhere. A heap of earth in the desert—an old town collapsed. What is buried in these mounds? Whole rooms still full of old things? We pass great flat valleys like in Colorado, where the black tents of the Kuchee nomads are set up, and herds of camels, sheep, goats, and horses are grazing. There is one group of tents like patchwork quilts—perhaps another tribe. We stopped in a cool, deep gorge and I washed my feet in the stream.

The mountains are now behind us and we're crossing a flat plain, not completely bare, for there are green islands here and there, walled orchards with pomegranates. I hope they're on the market already. Surely things ripen sooner in these hot, protected gardens. I get good vibrations here. Somewhere to the north, not very far, is the Soviet Union.

5:30. Mazar-i-Sharif. From the bus stop I took a horse carriage to the hotel, and discovered that the driver had taken me to the wrong hotel. I thought it looked a bit seedy and asked him if this was the Hotel Mazar and he said it was, though when a group of children raised their voices to correct him, he cursed them. So I asked around and after walking several dusty, unpaved blocks I came to a large and rambling run-down place that was obviously built with an idea of grandeur. And as at Bamian it seems all the rooms with bath are taken. So I'm in a dreary little room in the other wing.

I took a shower in the ramshackle hall bathroom and am lying down. It isn't so bad once you stop looking at it. It even has a shaded balcony. I ought to go out to the bazaar but am tired from little sleep and that bus ride, which was not, however, bad at all. The road was paved the whole way.

JULY 14. I slept out on the balcony last night but the sun hit me about six so I got up. The night never really got cool either and there were various kinds of bugs—bedbugs or fleas, I suspect, plus a few mosquitoes. From my balcony I looked enviously down in the hotel garden at a bed with a sleeping figure on it, on the side of the garden where the morning sun couldn't reach—a German woman guest sleeps out there. I'll look for a better place to sleep tonight.

I'm having breakfast at a very pleasant teahouse on the grounds of the shrine of Ali— bread and tea and a bunch of grapes that the man dipped in a tub of questionable water. The people here seem able to drink any water, even from the sewers, like animals do. And animals don't get sick from it. Why are we westerners so sensitive? Is it mental? The teashop is a cluster of wooden divans on the earth with a crude roof held up by stripped poles and some curtains. There is a little platform for two great brass samovars, a stove for cooking, and open shelves holding teapots and cups. Some cloths are hanging from the roof here and there, but loosely not to block wind, and miraculously there is a breeze here. It is pleasantly ramshackle, like everything in this country. The shrine gardens also look shabby and not taken care of. Everything is so dry, and there seems to be no place where there's water. One nice thing, the teashops here have very handsome carpets on their divans.

With its formal gardens the shrine sits in the middle of the town plaza like a sacred elephant. The setting was designed according to a grandiose scheme that was never fulfilled. The plan to build the streets fronting the square in a uniform architecture was never carried out to completion and construction of a number of the buildings was stopped half-way up and they stand unfinished, waiting for ...what? Authorization? Money? The tomb of Ali, the fourth *caliph* worshiped by the Shiites, is one of the holiest sites of Shia Islam, though Ali was not buried in Mazar-i-Sharif. He was actually buried in Baghdad, but it is believed by the faithful that his body was miraculously transported here. It does feel like a very holy place.

There are Russian women to be seen on the streets here, pale-skinned and housewifey in figure—like German hausfraus. They wear conventional, style-less print dresses, harlequin sun glasses, beauty parlor hairdos. Aside from them, there are few women to be seen, even totally veiled. The old customs rule here.

Walking around this town, it's a dusty prospect. With the half-finished buildings on the square, and the roads unpaved and rutted, full of horses and taxis, it's like a frontier town. It's obvious that Mazar doesn't show its wonders right off. How I can stay here I don't know. A young man named Zalmai whom I met on the bus came along and we went to look at another hotel, which turned out to be clean and pleasant. A large group of hippie-types were crowded into one room listening to a guitarist. The disadvantage is that they won't rent me a room by myself, so I'd have to share with someone. And even if it's cleaner and more modern than mine, the rooms are smaller and perhaps airless. With all the hashish-smoking hippies I'm afraid to move there since I'm so square.

Zalmai and I went into a rug shop and there was a very nice Bokhara, a big one, but the man asked 26,000 Afs. for it, which is ridiculous. It's an antique unfortunately, which allows them to ask anything. Even if new carpets are cheaper in Mazar, old ones are more expensive, just as I was told in Kabul. I'm coming back tomorrow and offering 2,000 for it and will see what happens. Zalmai then invited me to go smoke hashish with him, but I'm still shaky from the last time and turned down the invitation.

But now that it's dark it's cooler and the hotel garden that a little while ago looked dry and dusty has been sprinkled with water and seems fresh. A lot of the streets are also sprinkled in the evening which makes a big improvement. The carpet in my room is lovely. They are going to move the bed outside on the balcony so I can sit on the carpet inside. I'm going to eat here at the hotel tonight—one of the servants went with me to a melon vendor and we chose a melon for my dessert.

Tonight's meal at the hotel was greasy and only redeemed by the melon I bought. Two English boys who said they were in the English equivalent of our Peace Corps in Pakistan and on their way home were also eating in the dining room and afterwards joined me at my table, and then we had tea in the garden in the darkness. They're on their way back to England after a year's service and are on a tight budget. So they were upset when the bill came to 30 Afs. which is high for what we had, but usual in hotels. They have a room just below mine for 20 Afs. Cheaper—I should have bargained with the manager when I arrived.

11:00 AM. This morning when I visited the shrine of Ali I had an overwhelming desire to cry again. Why do holy places move me so? The building is basically undistinguished but is completely covered with tiles in various patterns making it glorious. It also feels right taking off your shoes before going in, though I wasn't allowed into the central room where the actual tomb is.

I also looked at old rugs in a number of shops in the rug bazaar but the good ones are very expensive. A merchant explained the bare spots in the woven pile as a result of people eating on the rugs, and the insects eating away the wool where food fell. I don't think it's possible for me as a foreigner to get a fair price. Besides, now that I've learned how to scratch the back of the rugs with my fingernails to see how tight the weave is, a trick all the rug people do, the dealers have become wary that I'm a professional.

This city is so dry and dusty and hot it shocks the senses. I wanted to go to Balkh, the great ruined city, but surely it's impossible in this heat. I used to be able to stay cool by keeping very still, but I seem to have lost the trick. I think I'd better take it easy in my room till late afternoon. I've bought bread, tomatoes, and a melon for lunch. Perhaps it would be wiser to go to the teahouse by the shrine to sleep after lunch—there was a breeze there earlier.

I've had such delicious melons here. The word fruit practically means melon here and many people walk around holding one. There are several varieties. The two kinds I've eaten so far are nothing like American melons—they're crisp and green and not really sweet, but refreshing.

Twilight. This is the hour to see the shrine. The tiles come alive and against the luminous sky the architecture makes sense. The blue dome gets bigger and floats in the air. The dust has died down and the flowers in the garden glow in the half-light. Even the buildings around the square lose their tackiness.

I'm sitting by a dry pool in the garden of the shrine hoping those fountains get turned on. How delicious the spray would be, the sound of water. Thank God twilight has come. The day was like fire. I stayed in until five but even then it was awful. I used the time studying Farsi. I find myself going through the whole Farsi book now instead of bogging down in one chapter, but tend to skip over the verbs which are jaw breakers.

How I love the shrine tonight. Suddenly the mountains show above the town, and bare as they are they still lend some interest to the rather squalid, tacky scene. I even like Mazar, impossible as it is. Perhaps I should stay on awhile, not go home until next Friday on the bus. Of course, the plane on Thursday afternoon would cost so little, nine dollars.

JULY 15. I've come to Balkh, a village near Mazar that is on the site of the ancient city of the same name called The Mother of Cities. I took a cab from Mazar with seven passengers for 10 Afs. each. The plain is dotted with ruined towns, one of which seemed perfectly preserved in its walls. I'm wearing my turban outside for the first time today and to my chagrin it came apart in the cab because of the wind, so I stuffed it into my sack. I still don't know how to wind it on properly.

Modern Balkh is now a country town, pleasanter than Mazar because it is green and leafy. It's shaped like a wheel, the hub being a park with a brilliantly-tiled ancient building in the center, and the ruins spread out enigmatically in all directions. There's even a hotel, though it doesn't look like there are any tourists at all. It's good for my Farsi, for no one here speaks English, but I'm attracting too much attention as the only tourist.

Around the gorgeous ruin in the park (part of a palace, a mosque?) are holy men, for this is a sacred place and a site of dervish pilgrimage. I picked up some fragments of tile around the ruin—it's still falling apart—a tile of sky-blue glaze, and a fragment of lapis lazuli color, the intense royal blue.

I walked out beyond the village and surveyed the countryside that is mostly desolate ruins. They are vast and nothing seems excavated. Great parts of the walls of the ancient city still stand and even some buildings. Beautiful glazed shards lie about, some with patterns, often of the heavenly blue. Some men were digging up earth and putting it in wheelbarrows, and as they dug, pottery fragments fell around. They probably come across a lot of artifacts.

There was a grove of trees with a well and sacred tombs where people were praying, so I went and drank the risky water—in the heat it's impossible to resist. The grove was surrounded by marijuana plants seemingly growing wild. Perhaps there's a hashish factory there too and they throw the seeds around. I didn't stay in the grove because I didn't feel welcome, perhaps because there were women there.

I climbed a commanding hill to look around at the ruins. There was a nomad encampment in one direction, which means dangerous dogs, so I couldn't go there. And on the other side a swamp with a colony of reed cutters. The old city must have had a lake within its walls that clogged up once it was destroyed. The sun was getting to me so I walked back to town.

My turban has created quite a stir. I think people are pleased I've adopted something of Afghanistan. I want to get a set of their clothes next. It will be cooler. On one of the radial streets, I stopped and sat with a tailor who had his sewing machine set up on the sidewalk making a shirt. A crowd gathered of course and one man gave me some plums. The tailor says he would make me a native shirt and pants suit for 30 Afs. In three hours. But I don't want to wait.

On another street I stopped and tried to speak with a dervish, but didn't get very far except to learn he was of the Naqshbandi order and that there were many dervishes here. It's a holy place for them. He wore hippie beads and coins on his bare chest, and had a beard but a shaven head. He had strange polyps growing from his ears. He asked me if I smoked hashish (I can understand that much Farsi now). When I said no, he said good.

I returned to Mazar in a taxi. I first got into a truck which was waiting to collect a full load of people, but it took so long people kept leaving in disgust, so when I saw a share taxi waiting I got into it. It filled up quickly with its seven passengers, and we left. We passed again the dead town with the intact walls.

After Balkh which was so nice, Mazar is impossibly dusty. The water I drank in Balkh has made my stomach hurt. I'll have to eat some yoghurt which is the best medicine for it. I wish I dared eat some of the local ice cream. I wonder how long it would take me to get accustomed to the local germs and be able to drink the water and eat the ice cream.

I tried on some locally-manufactured shoes, almost like wooden shoes in shape, but they are very hard. I suppose once they are broken in they're good to walk in on these stony tracks. But I foresee aching feet and blisters for days. Maybe I should have some made to order in Kabul. Soft suede with rubber soles, in this local style. Nothing I wear seems right for walking here.

I've bought my ticket back to Kabul for Friday. Why didn't I buy it for

Saturday? I could have had an extra day here. But on Sunday I must start getting a new visa. I've gotten quite used to Friday being the sabbath and Saturday and Sunday being work days.

At a tea shop I spoke to an enchantingly handsome young mullah who invited me to come to his *khanega* Thursday night for an all night prayer meeting. It's in a nearby village. We sat holding hands and gazing into each other's eyes. I presume as a mullah he teaches children. He is twenty-four and unmarried, which is unusual.

This afternoon I had a long talk with my neighbor in the hotel, a Viennese publisher of educational reprints. He and his friend, an older man, are always in their room lying around wearing only underwear briefs because of the heat. They are going to join an expedition into the Hindu Kush on a mapping project and are waiting for a plane to Faizabad. He doesn't think there is anything here worth seeing, and even my mentioning Balkh didn't excite his interest. He depressed me with his utter dismissal of Mazar.

My talk with the mullah also depressed me for some reason. We had a sweet encounter, but so many people stood around. I'm getting a little fed up with being such an object of public curiosity. Will I have the nerve to go to the *dervish* meeting Thursday night?

Coming back to the hotel, I met the manager who seems to me to be a chiseler. He says my room is 110 Afs. a night (with service) and more expensive than the room below me because it is on the second floor. Downstairs they're cheaper. Then I bought five postcards of Balkh from the hotel postcard stand. Postcards are always 5 Afs. and I gave him 30 Afs. Instead of giving me my 5 Afs. change, he said they cost 6 Afs. each. He has a quick mind.

I've finally had *mast* (yoghurt) to eat but after the first few mouthfuls it gave me the creeps. It was too watery. I'll have some fruit before bed and that will be enough. I was charged 12 Afs. for the *mast* and I think it's a penalty for not ordering pilau or kebabs as a tourist should. They disapprove of my way of eating. Today is my day for being gypped. Still, it's all such petty gyppery, in our money terms. In theirs it is serious.

Strange how some men also hold a cloth in their teeth, like women do in Iran to veil their faces.

In the local dialect, the people don't pronounce the V in words as we do, but as W, like in Latin.

Some men carry handsome striped cotton or silk coats that they fold very carefully, or wear over their shoulders, cape-style, with the unnaturally long sleeves hanging decoratively. The lining is always a certain tiny flower-print cloth. The winter coats are similar but padded with cotton.

Later. I'm sitting on a doorstep under a streetlamp. I don't want to go to bed so early— it's too hot. I seem to have attracted the attention of someone. He has stopped on the road and is looking at me attentively. I can't tell anything about him in the darkness.

The shrine looks especially beautiful -- at night its size increases to noble proportions. But during the day it's magical the way the colors change continually -- there are such a variety of patterns. The tiles at Balkh were mosaics, not painted glazed motifs like modern tiles, designed to make a repeated pattern. Each color was cut to shape to fit into the pattern. Of course the final effect is the same.

JULY 16. I've come to a marvelous market town, Tashkoran, about an hour away from Mazar to the south in the desert. It's also called Khulm. Tashkoran is a desert town and a dry warm wind is blowing. I'm eternally thirsty.

I got here in a small pick-up truck with a canvas top and benches along the sides. It held eight people, each paying 20 Afs. Three of the passengers besides me were westerners. One of them, an English boy, was being very lordly, telling off the beggar woman, who stood behind the truck pleading with her blind eyes, and then the driver's assistant when he tried to collect his fare. He was a student at Kent University, but was more like a colonial officer putting up with the bloody buggers of natives in some remote outpost of the empire. There was also a Dane, a young architect, on his way to Kashmir. And a French boy from Lille who was going to Australia to work -- they are impossibly romantic, the French. The boys were all dressed in the native pajama-type clothes which they had gotten by exchanging their own, but they didn't excite the appreciation my wearing a turban did.

We discussed the rumor going around of a boat from Japan to Alaska that costs $40. That would make it possible to bum around the whole world, since the Pacific is the big barrier for world travelers. There's hardly any way to cross it cheaply, outside of working your way across.

The Dane said he wanted to go to Nuristan because the people there are reputed to be Aryans, descendents of ancient Greeks, remnants of Alexander's army who settled there, so we all (meaning, we Aryans) should be interested. I replied acidly that I wasn't an Aryan. It's true that westerners are fascinated by the Nuristanis who only recently were converted from some so-called primitive religion to the Muslim faith. There are no roads in and you have to go by horseback over mountain trails to get there. I've heard that in winter when it snows and they are completely isolated from the outside world they revert to their pagan practices. Of course it must be a cool place to go in summer and remote, but I'm not sure I share the usual fascination.

Another story I've heard is that a foreign boy visiting the Nuristanis was locked in his room while they performed some forbidden rite and he claimed to have smelled strange meat cooking which he discovered was human flesh. Perhaps an old wives' tale. A place with no roads is always interesting. You need special permission to go there. In any case, I'm not sure I'm up to traveling by horseback.

Tashkoran is situated just before the mountains and has impressive ruins of its own outside the present village, but they don't seem to have any special attraction for tourists or pilgrims. But it does have a famous, and picturesque, bazaar two days a week. Camels go through the streets carrying things. I looked at some old coins and other objects in a shop near the Silversmiths' Quarter. The man said they were found nearby. A lot of it was Greek. A piece of pottery with drawings scratched into it—animals, a head or two, Greek words—it seemed genuine. But perhaps they keep manufacturing the stuff. The coins did look newly-minted. Still, this place hasn't enough tourists for that.

A purple silk, padded coat with intense embroidery around the neckline was offered to me for 1000 Afs. Pottery with blue glaze only on the inside of the jugs and vases but with a little dripping over the rim. Why didn't I buy a little blue-glazed oil lamp with a delicately molded spout? Or any of the local embroidery which is as good as Bokhara? Will I ever come back? I'm such a fool. I never buy.

The people have been especially friendly. Some men called me into a yard where a wild mountain goat was tied up. He had large curved horns and stood quietly looking at me with his pop-eyes. His doe, a classically delicate creature, was let loose. The children chased her and she bounded about like a little ballet dancer. I scratched the male's head and I think he liked it, but the children tended to be afraid of him, gentle as he was, and dart up and kick him or hit him with a stick and leap back. He lowered his horns and threatened them, but there was no harm in him.

I was sitting on the mats outside a teahouse along the lively stream that cuts through the bazaar, enjoying the refreshing sound of the water, when some students stopped out of curiosity. They kept asking me political questions that I discreetly refused to answer. They asked me if I saw any difference between Russia's or China's political system. I replied that they were both socialism. They laughed at my naiveté and said that Russia's was socialist imperialism and China's socialism. All the students were for socialism, they said, meaning I suppose that they were pro-China. They go to school in Mazar where they have a Peace Corps teacher for English. One of them said bitterly that this teacher hit him. When I told him I wanted to report him to my friend in Kabul who was an official in the Peace Corps and asked the man's name, he wouldn't give it to me and started to change the story, and got confused. I think he was afraid of the consequences.

A sweet old countryman sitting next to me refused to understand my outlandish Farsi, but gave me almonds to eat and insisted on paying for my tea.

In a melon market with heaps of melons lying on the ground I bought a small one. The vendor had three varieties but there are obviously many more. Mine was something like our cantaloupe. I also ate some fried pastries with onion grass filling called boloney, tomatoes of an unheard-of sweetness, sticky figs, tiny cherries, bread and tea. There was even grilled fish from the river, but I didn't trust it.

Tashkoran is just off the main road, so I walked back from the bazaar to the highway— or most of the way, before I was given a ride by a boy who had hired a horse and buggy. The driver wanted an extra 5 Afs. from me, but the boy wouldn't let me pay and we walked off ignoring the driver's protests. That's the way to do it here. When bargaining they will never agree to your final price, but if you put the money in their hand, take the merchandise, and walk off, it's usually acceptable. You have to make up your mind and do it.

Now I'm waiting at the bus stop at the highway for some kind of transportation back to Mazar. Once there, I'll go look for the swimming pool I've heard about but don't believe in. With the hot wind blowing the dust in my face, I'm glad for my turban, the loose end of which makes a good mask across the face, tucked into it on the other side.

I went swimming and it was magnificent. Yes, world, there is a swimming pool in Mazar, but it is unique. It's in the Park of Women, a place I hadn't thought of going before. Oddly, there were no women there at all as far as I can see. There was a large sports stadium—and by a grove of trees the pool, with a row of changing lockers. It's a plain cement tank, but all around the edge are wooden divans with carpets on them where men sit drinking tea and looking with amazement at the few people who swim.

The water isn't too cold or too clear—in fact there's a slime on the sides of the pool and the water has a murkiness that makes me question its source—but here it is an event to swim. And also soothing to the bites.

The men on the divans stared and stared as I swam—there were only one or two others in the water—so I did my fanciest crawl. A man called me over to his divan and as I held on to the edge of the pool he handed me down a tiny glass of tea. When I got out of the water with my body shining and the suit clinging, I felt admired from all sides. I stayed until dusk. How I wish I'd discovered this earlier in my stay!

I've felt better about my body here than anywhere ever. In my frequent showers I had a sense that my body was well-shaped and my genitals lively and large. Maybe it's the local posture that has affected me and given me a better image of myself. Or is it something deeper? The holy vibes?

Walking back to the hotel, I saw in front of one shop a hawk sitting on a peg with only a cord around its leg. Further on was a family of rabbits free on the ground, grazing but staying close to home. And a fox was tied to another shop front. So many people have pet birds in cages or even hopping around the floor of a shop. They have an affinity for wild animals. It's only dogs here that have a curse on them.

Who could have taught these people that the way to address a foreigner is by calling Mistáh (with the accent on the second syllable)? Maybe the British. Or they think it's the equivalent of Monsieur. But come to think of it, how do you attract the attention of someone? But it gets irritating when everybody calls Mistáh at you down the street. As if you're there for their interest rather than your own. But they're sweet. They're just happy if you come over and look at their goods, even if you don't buy.

The floor boy in the hotel says that Afghan women don't smoke hashish but eat it in candy.

JULY 17. A little boy sitting near me has a pierced ear with one earring. I noticed Zalmai had a pierced ear but doesn't wear a wire in it. Within such a short period of time, Zalmai's seventeen years, many people have dropped the old ways and have gone as western as they are able. This little boy also has blue painted or tatooed on his lower eyelids. Little girls often have henna on their palms, like in Morocco.

I ate some figs yesterday but with trepidation. How I long for pomegranates, which I see in gardens fattening on the bushes, but not in the market.

Every Muslim country seems to have its own version of the skull cap, turban, blowy clothes. Could they be considered particularly Muslim clothes?

I did an exercise of praying while I had a hard-on, thinking that if I concentrated hard enough on the prayer I might come off when I got to Amen. I must try this when smoking hash.

I'm not sure I should go back to the Tourist Hotel in Shar-i-Nau. It's too expensive. The Jamil is cheaper and almost as new, but downtown in an ugly neighborhood, in the row of new buildings fronting the park, gimcracky modern. Still, it's a convenient location. The Faiz is near the bazaar. The Ariana is convenient to the embassy and the rug bazaar, but such a dead neighborhood, near the royal palace. And it's government-run which makes me dubious.

5:30 PM. Kabul seems so cool and modern after Mazar. The bus ride between the two cities is sensational, the ancient desert world of the north, the great mountains dividing the country, with the Salang Pass through them, and the intense, lush valleys. We only made two stops on the way back, once for lunch and once for fruit, the same fruit stop on the way out. Boys bring baskets of grapes to the bus stop for sale. There was a brief melon stop too where the driver bought three melons. I think it was a place famous for melons and perhaps for low prices, for there were heaps of melons everywhere else but we passed them by.

This is a comfortable bus line, but you don't get the variety of people like the government bus which is a few cents cheaper and where you're all jammed in. The only interesting person on the bus was a boy sitting in front of me who said he was a Turkoman. So that is what all those semi-Chinese, Mongolian-looking people must be. It's also the third language of the country after Farsi and Pashtoon.

I'm back in my room on the garden at the Tourist Hotel and feel guilty about spending so much. I could move into one of the rooms in the old wing facing the street which are much cheaper. But I only plan to be here a few days for renewing my visa and getting my mail. Whoever had my room after I left must have been a junkie. There's a hypodermic needle in the toilet that won't flush down, and pieces of rubber tubing on the floor by the drain.

My whole body is spotted with bug bites and before going to my room, I shook out my valise and clothes on the lawn at the suggestion of the patron who begged me not to bring bugs into his hotel. I wonder how long it will take my bites to go away. I wish I knew what made them. I even got bites in the bus. Tonight I must eat well.

The floor boy is coveting, nay, lusting, after my transistor radio. I told him I couldn't sell it to him because it was a present from my father (which it was). But I think he'll find a way of getting it. There's a desperation in his eyes when he looks at it. He might steal it of course.

While I've been away I feel that all the people I knew have left town. It's that kind of a place. But it seems there are more long-haired foreigners on the streets than before. The tourist season is on. It's odd that there's not one long-haired Afghan boy to be seen. A few with long sideburns. But the young men look so modern here after Mazar. And the streets look clean. How my vision changes!

I feel considerably changed by Mazar. It made me feel more Jewish and good about being Jewish. I always liked being a Jew but felt indifferent toward the religion. And now I don't feel as desperate about being alone. One nice thing about this room, there's privacy.

Odd, my body seems so hideous to me here. I've gotten so thin. But in Mazar I felt good about myself. I'd better get out of Kabul as soon as possible. But first I must try to get a pair of shoes made, or find soft sandals. I can't seem to solve this problem of the right footwear.

What happened today to make me feel ugly? Was it just leaving Mazar and the shrine of Ali? I can understand the dervishes who dwell by the shrine. I'd like to be in a horse and carriage like in Mazar. I was so happy there. Was it the possibility of love?

JULY 18. The hashish last night was the strongest I've ever taken—it was frightening. What was in that hash I got from the wily manager? I never threw up from it before. In that book about peyote it said if you puke it means you have devils in you to puke out, and I'm certain that I have them in me.

Of course I was very tired last night, and it wasn't a good time to turn on, and I think I smoked too much of the hash. Also I was feeling low—a couple of strange experiences when I went out to dinner helped bring me down. I saw a boy I met on the bus from Kandahar who was unfriendly and made me feel rejected. Then I passed some men who called out "Mistah, touristi?" which must be a crack about foreigners, for a westerner behind me said, "Shut your dirty mouth, pig." What was dirty about what they said? "Che touristi" means roughly, How are you? I've heard other Afghanis say over and over "Touristi?" and laughing, and felt annoyed at the time that they kept repeating it. I must find out if there's a double entendre. But surely the foreigner behind me was being stupid and arrogant for reacting that way.

Then I went to buy a few cigarettes to make joints with. They cost two and a half afs. but the boy only gave me a quarter afghani in change instead of a half (25 puls instead of 50, since there are 100 puls to the afghani). I asked for the rest and he started giving me an argument that he was in the right, and another boy came up and supported him, so, offended, I gave him back the cigarettes, took my money and walked on, for I was not going to stay and fight over such a trifle. Their laughter followed me as I left and I felt angry and humiliated, especially since I had disliked the foreigner behind me for getting uptight. There I was becoming enraged by the boy cheating me of 1/4 Af. assuming I was a dumb foreigner who didn't know the difference. I should have stayed and played his silly game good-naturedly. Perhaps the foreigner was annoyed at being addressed as Mistah, and the familiarity of the overture.

Foreigners do have contempt for much about this place. Someone said with a smile that the Afghans believe eating lemons is the best remedy for stomach problems, as if it were ridiculous. I replied that they are right and told how in Greece the remedy for the runs is boiled rice with lemon squeezed over it, which I seemed to be eating most of the time I was there in 1949.

I'm at the Khyber for breakfast, where I always go when I'm insecure. The fountain outside is a blessing. I feel shaky and must be hung over. Nobody seems friendly today and I can't get a waiter. The view of the fountain is partly blocked by a camper. My head certainly is funny, achy over the eyes. I feel tottery, dizzy. How can I smoke just a little of that hash? The pipes are too large and a cigarette is too much. I could perhaps make one-fourth of a cigarette, but even that is probably too much, strong as this stuff is.

Ah, the VW has moved and if I could cut down the pine trees partly blocking my view of the waters I'd be content.

I just don't have the nerve to wear my *lunghi* (turban) into the American Embassy when I go for my mail. It's something they could never understand. And it's precisely because of that that the Afghans appreciate it so.

JULY 20. I woke up before six and am lying in bed full of a strange vibration in my body, a weakness. Anxiety? Hopelessness? It is even hard to write. Yet I've got to go to the police for my passport. And I must pursue the wrapping paper problem today to mail my purchases home.

It's interesting about the new craze to drive from Europe across Asia, as though Europe had suddenly discovered that it's part of the same landmass as Asia. Psychologically, we were brought up denying that Asia was connected to Europe. Why was Asia made another continent?

Later. I got my new visa which will be valid until August 18. Surely they made a small mistake, for it should be good for 30 days, but I didn't dare say anything. You know not to here. They told me I would also need an exit visa before leaving. A tourist is not supposed to need one, but I'd better get it. The police, like police everywhere, put on a very intimidating manner. Several officers had to sign my passport, and the final one was the chief himself. It was scary going into his office. What a contemptuous look he had on his face as he put his elaborate signature on.

I actually mailed the package, the *chadri*. It wasn't impossibly hard to do, and only cost fifty cents. But I shouldn't have tied it up before it was inspected. The postmaster who was called to approve it looked it over suspiciously, asking what was in the package. When I said a *chadri* for a woman in America he also laughed heartily at the idea. Now that I've sent my first package, I ought to try to send a rug. That would be the real test.

Walking to the post office I saw flocks of sheep grazing on the grass along the streets, turkeys and geese loose, a donkey man. And passed by the American ambassador's residence with his own vegetable garden. Yesterday, when a camel train passed me in the market, it struck me what an unusual city this is. Men ride donkeys through the streets, even in this fancy side of town, and sheep are herded through the streets, perhaps to slaughterhouses. A horseman rode by me not using stirrups or bit, right across from the American Embassy. That's quite common here. The bit now seems to me to be cruel and unnecessary. Riding a donkey looks quite pleasant. You have a little stick to tap it with to indicate where you want it to go.

A man was selling mulberries by the road. I longed to eat some but didn't dare for I was sure the water he was washing them in was from the open gutter, or even city tap water. Yesterday I wanted carrot juice from a street-juicer but he too was washing the carrots in the open drain.

I've seen quite a bit of coolie labor. Their carts loaded with provisions have pneumatic tires, but still it looks like hard work for a man to pull one.

Evening. I'm in my pleasant garden kebab restaurant again. I ordered eggplant with my kabobs, but the word for eggplant and the word for tomato seem, inexplicably, to be the same. So I have a plate of sliced tomatoes instead.

There really is no tipping in this country. And people are willing to do things for you. Like any restaurant will prepare and serve you a melon you bring in yourself.

My new sandals have already started to rub, so before they made blisters I treated myself to a cab to the American Embassy and there was a letter, making it worth the 20 Af s. (Last time the cabbie insisted the standard fare was 30 Afs.) My driver turned out to be the young man who drove the American family and me to Band-i-Amir and the cab was the same Opal we all pushed up the hills that time. We agreed that his car was good for Kabul but not for Band-i-Amir. He talked at a great rate and I understood practically nothing, but he didn't notice.

I was early to pick up the new suit of Afghan clothes that I ordered from a tailor yesterday—he said it would take six meters of cloth for the long shirt and baggy pants—so I explored the bazaar for an hour or two. First I came across a street of jewelry-making shops in a place where I'm sure no tourist ever strays, a hopelessly filthy and poor part of town right behind the Khyber restaurant. But the silver jewelry was fine, traditional stuff. I didn't dare ask prices or I would have been hounded. Then by the river I passed a donkey driver and said he had a beautiful animal. He offered to sell him to me, so I asked the price. He said 10,000 Afs. but came down to 8000 almost immediately, still high for a donkey, I think. I really would like one, but wouldn't know how to take care of it, where to keep it, how to sell it again, and how to leave it without breaking my heart. I already loved this beautiful white donkey.

I asked one of the men there what he had on his eyes which were rimmed in blue-tattoo, paint, medicine? He was a beautiful man and the blue line around his eyes made him devastating, which may have been its function. His answer was a word I didn't know but felt his hostility to my question, which I admit was impertinent.

I crossed the river and found a gun and gun supplies area. Then an area of tailor shops where I stopped at one stall to listen to a man singing marvelous though endless songs and playing a two-string lute while another man beat the open top of a water jug with one palm and the side with his scissors handle in the proper rhythm. The tailors kept on working through the recital.

A crowd gathered—one of my problems is that every time I stop to talk with someone, and that is often, I have an audience, even for intimate moments. Everyone asks me if I smoke hashish, and when I started telling a watch repairman today about my experience with bad hash we suddenly had an audience around us. Of course we were speaking English which they probably didn't understand. This watch dealer said he knew a way to send hashish safely through the mails, by putting it in with a box of glassware covered with labels saying "Fragile" and "This Side Up." I told him I wouldn't risk it and that many post offices had dogs trained to smell it. The letter I got today from a friend was full of warnings not to carry any across the border. A *Life* magazine article about Americans in jail in exotic countries for drug smuggling scared her. It said American authorities can't do anything about it. Of course they can't. But I suspect that they instigate the arrests, most of which are nationals of other countries, and the few Americans who are caught can't be given special treatment. But I bet a liberal shmearing with *baksheesh* in the right places would get them out.

Going in the direction of my tailor's, I came across sellers of *jitaks*, the long striped coats with the long dangling sleeves that are rarely used. The more expensive ones have sleeves of an unusable length, as long as the coat itself. They were asking 200 Afs. for rayon, and about 800 Afs. for silk ones. I liked the green and purple stripes best. Very handsome but overpriced. There was also a heavy brown homespun wool coat from Bamian— I didn't see anything like that for sale when I was there.

I picked up my blue suit and went home, with a stop at my Bamian rug dealers on the way (they still won't come down to my price) and a look-in at the Khyber. I talked to a foreign girl who was just bumming around, waiting for a lift to somewhere else—a resident of the Najib Hotel, naturally.

I tried on my suit and found the shirt a little tight at the neckline but otherwise beautiful and comfortable. From the way it's cut I don't see how it can be fixed. But I can wear it anyway. I tried on my turban with it and except for my long hair I look pretty authentic. The long-haired Afghanis have straight black hair cut severely across like Amazonian Indians. If I had a vest and a kind of table cloth for a shawl over one shoulder, I'd be complete. But I don't have the nerve yet to go out in this outfit.

The wind has been blowing, a cool one happily, but could one really expect that all that stuff blowing into your eyes won't produce a serious infection? There are so many blind people, or half-blind, perhaps from the dust. I'm getting quite callous at brushing aside crippled beggars. A boy comes on, producing tears on cue. They thrust their deformity at you, the stump of an arm, or their blind eyes. One woman I could swear had her eyes rolled up in her head to look blind.

On my way out of the restaurant the young man in the cashier's booth said he was going to give me hashish tomorrow night. I think he meant that we would have a small party together, for the offer of hashish is often an overture of friendship. I've been offered hashish about six times today alone, not for sale, but for free. The watch seller said they smoke hash mixed with opium but that it's too strong for westerners. Perhaps that was what the manager gave me. I'm not too anxious to turn on at this point. But if someone is there to hold on to, perhaps it would be all right.

I asked at the embassy about going to Jerusalem overland through Iraq and Jordan, but they said it was impossible. I'll have to go through Cyprus. That means going to southern Turkey and finding a boat to Cyprus and then one to Israel. Perhaps I could go through Iran and Iraq (or Syria?), by train to Lebanon, and then get a boat to Cyprus. Possibly through Damascus and

Baghdad on that route. I'll ask at the Turkish Embassy what they think.

JULY 21. Yesterday on the bus I ran into a boy who worked at the Park Hotel where I stayed when I first arrived. I had paid 250 Afs. a night, but he told that now that the hotel is officially open the room rate was raised to 600 Afs. I wanted to say that I hoped their salaries were tripled too. He was one of the boys who studied English painfully, touchingly, sitting in the hall, and who told me he and one other boy there liked the guests,, implying that the rest of the employees did not, and it is true that the others weren't helpful.

He was carrying a guest's dirty clothes loose in his arms to be washed, I thought he said to his room somewhere, but surely he lives at the hotel. To his family? Why am I thinking of him first thing upon awakening this morning? Because of his poverty? His simpleness? What is his ambition in life, and is anything possible for him here? Will he fall into bitterness? He looks like he'll be old in no time. Could he possibly earn enough to buy a wife? Does anyone tip in hotels here? I don't think they do. It's heart-wrenching that a poor boy like this shakes your hand goodbye with shining eyes. So many people are impossibly sweet to me here.

Maybe I should go somewhere outside the city. Yet it is so cool these days, it couldn't be lovelier.

Later. I'm sitting at the Khyber, for if I keep walking around in these sandals I'm going to get blisters. I wonder if I dare go back to the shoe shop and have the sandals adjusted again? I'd better go back to the hotel and change into shoes.

I watched chickens being slaughtered in the street. Before he cuts its throat, the man steps on the outspread wings. That keeps the headless bird from flopping about and spurting blood all over. The wings of successive chickens are spread over the previous one, so there is a little pile of carcasses all pinned down.

The exchange rate is 83 Afs. to the dollar. Should I change money today? Go to the rug bazaar? Have heel straps put on the sandals? I'll just sit here for awhile until my inner state calms down and a course of action seems clear, if action is in fact necessary at all. I'm a little weak—an attack of diarrhea this morning has unmanned me. And homesick. The mail from home was disturbing. I really need an Afghan friend, partly to help me in my daily activities, and partly for company. It's hard to live here and he would teach me how. Do I want to stay here in Afghanistan? How ironic, I write to everybody how happy I am here and then I'm miserable.

The fountain outside has stopped for the day and now the square is dull and too bright, too hot.

Later. I'm sitting in a little teashop across from a movie house, feeling slightly feverish so I'm skipping lunch and all I'm having is bread and tea, which I believe is curative. Do I feel well enough to go to the movie?

I had gone back to my room to change into shoes when my dervish friends dropped in unexpectedly. Now I'm committed to dinner and all-night prayers Thursday night. They seem kind people. I modeled my new clothes for them and they said I looked beautiful in them. Dare I go out in this outfit?

A western suit of clothes is quite a mark of prestige here, and in this modern neighborhood the majority of men are at least in a pair of slacks and sport shirt. The styles of the suits are still that trim, boxy, handsome style the French long ago abandoned for the long, shaped jacket that makes everyone look foppish. There don't seem to be any ready-to-wear suits in the shops, but there are loads of tailors. Actually, in the bazaar on Jadi-Maiwand, the main avenue of the old town, there are racks of coats and vests for sale, to be worn over the traditional clothes.

I saw a naked little boy and he was uncircumcised, so perhaps they do the operation later. It is surely healthier done later.

A little flock of black sheep with splotches of pink paint on their foreheads is going by. The ram leads elegantly and the boy drives them from behind.

This morning I ran into the young furrier who was in the cab from Istalif and made lewd suggestions to me. Today he was considerably shabbier looking and made no invitation except to lead me into his shop to buy. But I thought everything uninteresting and felt a general lack of talent. Later I met the young Frenchman who lost his locks and beard at the border. He has delayed his departure because of a bout of diarrhea. He and a friend were on their way to the money bazaar to buy rupees since they'll be leaving for Pakistan and India soon.

I'm seeing an Indian movie and it's a long enough saga to require an intermission, which we are having now. The orchestra where I'm sitting costs 12 Afs. and the balcony 20. But the balcony is very far away from the screen, if more desirable. It seems like a legitimate theatre with an orchestra pit and numbered seats, with a portrait of the king and another of the queen on either side of the stage.

The movie is about a modern playboy prince who in obedience to his father marries the old-fashioned girl chosen for him, but leaves her right after the wedding without consummating the marriage and goes to England to live it up in nightclubs. The traditional wife goes a little crazy from grief, runs away, and when she collapses in the rain, is picked up by an older wealthy man who for some reason adopts her as a daughter. (In the talky parts it's harder to follow since it's dubbed into Farsi.) He brings her up to date by getting her a teased hairdo, and French and dancing lessons, and buys her a chic wardrobe instead of saris. Then she goes to England where her husband meets and falls in love with her without recognizing her in her new garb.

It's a good story and can obviously be stretched out with complications indefinitely. It's completely filmed in India including the scenes in London. The extras playing English people were obviously selected from the foreign colony in Bombay—they say you can earn 40 rupees a day there as an extra in the movies. These were an odd mixture of obvious hippie potheads with conventional English residents. Some of the bearded men with stoned eyes did not quite fit into the old-fashioned nightclub scenes with their floorshows of chorus girls.

My first outing in full costume has been successful. When the wind blows it feels so good, all that light cotton rippling over you. I should have worn my *lunghi* also. But I seem to have gotten a few new bites in the movie house.

JULY 23.   Last night as I was coming from the hotel kitchen with a bottle of drinking water and a glass of ice cubes to take to my room, three long-haired boys in the dining room motioned me to sit down with them. Two of them were English and one an American from Colorado. They asked me for cigarettes and I said I had some in my room, so they came up. My room amazed them. They were staying in a small hotel somewhere—they didn't even know the name of it— where the beds cost 20 Afs. (a quarter), but they were sleeping on the floor for half that. So I seemed to them to be living in incredible luxury, paying $2.50 a night for my beautiful room with bath.

I couldn't invite them to eat with me—I had only a small piece of bread to go with the tomatoes, cheese, and fruit. I also sensed they were the staying type, so we stood and talked.

After they left, I felt I'd made a mistake—I should have shared what I had. They said they loved the Russian cigarettes with the long filters I gave them.

I'm at the bank. Is the *karakul* hat many men wear a sign of prestige? One step up from the turban? The foreigners look a ratty lot compared to the stiffly formal bank employees. At the foreign exchange window the teller says he lived and went through high school in New York where his father was in the UN delegation from Afghanistan. He talks excitedly about his life there to the blonde girl from Queens standing ahead of me. He worked at Chase Manhattan in New York.

A French girl asked him for part of her traveler's check in Afghanis and part in dollars. He then asked me if I wanted all of my check in Afghanis, so I also took part in Afghanis and part in dollars. But I suspect he's allowing us to do this in order to impress us. Another day the regulations could forbid it.

I'm dizzy again today. A young man in the waiting line asked me what hospital a foreigner could go to. I told him I heard Avicenna was the best and asked him what was wrong. He said he had amoebic dysentery and was vomiting blood, that standing up was difficult and sometimes he nearly fainted. I'm scared. What if my dizziness is the beginning of something like that? Stomach problems here are terrifying. Today my stomach still doesn't feel good. I'd better not eat until I'm hungry. But what about dinner tonight at Abdul Rahim's house? As a guest, I'll be expected to eat like a horse.

In the bank, I also spoke with a young Afghani journalist who's going to Canada and, he hopes, to the U.S. He was getting preferential treatment at the bank, yet he seemed a humble person, almost beaten. He said he worked on printing machinery, and also wrote news and commentary, so perhaps he was mostly a writer. That could be a risky job in this country. He asked me all sorts of questions about working in Canada and the U.S. And about money—prices there sound so enormous to the Afghans. A visa for the U.S. is almost impossible to get unless you buy a round-trip ticket and can show it. So he's going to Canada first, where the regulations are less strict. He'll fly Aeroflot from Moscow to Montreal, and since he has relatives in Moscow he'll buy the ticket there, paying rubles, and the fare will be a lot cheaper than buying it here. He's also going to take little items of clothing to sell in Moscow. It's amazing how people manage in every situation. I agreed that it might be easier to come to the U.S. for a visit from Canada, and suggested that he could even apply for an immigration visa once he was in Canada if he wanted. But I saw he was afraid. Obviously, he's been through a rough time and the authorities terrify him. I felt he wouldn't have an easy time of it in America. I wonder what his real story is? He might have been just out of jail. But why the respectful treatment at the bank?

After the bank, I went to the embassy for my mail. I was walking away slowly, under the shady trees along the avenue, reading my letters, when a boy on a bicycle stopped and talked with me. He said he was a student and has American teachers in math and English, but his English was minimal so we talked in Farsi. His father is a farmer and grows grain—*juwar*, a word I don't know. When we parted he kissed me on the lips, then quickly kissed me again as though he liked the first one and couldn't resist. How tender he was! And right in front of the American Embassy!

Later, a Hindu (you can tell by the way they wear their turbans) asked me if I wanted to change money, and I stopped to talk with him. He said with a smile that all the moneychangers and people in that line were Hindus. It was funny for a Jew to be told that.

I'm again at the Khyber restaurant, and couldn't resist buying Jello. How I love it, even warm, as they serve it here. Their tea is Lipton's teabags. At the movie there was an ad on the screen for Lipton's teabags the other night, as well as an ad for cigarettes, showing a man in evening clothes lighting a gowned woman's cigarette with a fancy lighter—incredible to see such a thing here where women are totally veiled.

In ordinary tea shops you get your own pot of tea, often for as little as half an Afghani (less then a penny) without sugar, as I drink it, or 1 Af. if you take sugar—the Khyber and my hotel charge five. You usually pour a little tea around the outside rim of your glass and swish some around inside it and throw it on the floor—presumably this sterilizes it, but is also like a libation. When you finish each glass of tea you empty the dregs into a special dish or throw them on the floor. The tea isn't always leaves but sometime odd little granules. You can order either green or black, and in some poor tea shops fresh tea is added to old dregs, or just water is added and you have to send it back.

People here are always asking me if America is good, and I always say it is good, "khoob ist," but that the government is both good and bad. It does good things and it does bad things like all governments. One man said Nixon was bad and Johnson was bad, so I guess they can be read clearly from halfway around the world. I just laughed loudly at the remark. I say I'm a guest here and can't talk politics. The truth is my Farsi isn't good enough for more than these elementary things.

JULY 24.   Last night I found Abdul's house in one of the oldest parts of the city without much trouble, and on the way discovered the used-clothing-and-shoes bazaar in a maze of alleys, and then a market of fruit being set up for tomorrow in a large field, with stalls being built and piles of melons on woven mats. I also came across a few antique shops, improbably set here in this neighborhood where surely few tourists ever wander through.

I was wearing full Afghan costume, my baggy bloomer pants, long shirt, and turban. It was my first experience "passing." It felt odd not to be called after down the street or hardly noticed. I look exactly like these people. But when I asked the price of a carpet in my clumsy Farsi I was immediately spotted and given the tourist price.

Abdul's house is traditional. You are let in through a door in a high wall and go through a courtyard. The living room has woven mats over the ceiling, which must be plastered with mud and straw—a really handsome ceiling—and peeled tree trunk beams holding it all up. The room has no furniture, just pillows and rugs. I sensed the women's activity beyond the cloth hung over the door at the end of the room, and actually caught a glimpse of a dress now and then. Dinner was a banquet on the floor, spread like a picnic. Besides my friends, there were several male relatives. Each of us was served a sheet of the good *nan*. There were heaping platters of rice and the traditional side dishes of lamb stew and eggplant to go with it, and bowls of melon chunks and grapes. I went ahead and ate.

After dinner my friends took me on a long, complicated route through dank alleys to the Chishti dervish house for a look at their Thursday night meeting. This was just a few blocks from the center of the old city and I didn't understand at first why we took such a devious route to get there. Without my friends I could never have found it, for it's at the dead end of an unobtrusive alley, and the doorway certainly doesn't look like a doorway. You stoop down under a low archway of stones, waist-high, then climb a dark stairway and come out on a roof-terrace overlooking a small interior courtyard. The roof-terrace led into the large main hall, where the dervishes were already singing and playing instruments in one corner of the room, but as it was already packed with seated men we sat outside on the roof where along with many other seated figures we could hear and see pretty well through the large open door and windows. I couldn't see the whole orchestra but it sounded like Ravi Shankar-type music played on the same kind of instruments. They must have been singing prayers, each of which went on for a long time. One old, old bearded man seemed to be the master dervish. This meeting didn't seem to involve audience participation—besides the musicians, everyone else was just listening.

My friends told me not to speak under any circumstances, for it might have been dangerous for me. I sensed this was not an activity open to outsiders, and perhaps an illegal meeting. My outfit made me nearly invisible, luckily. If I were wearing a vest and had a cloth for a shawl and weren't dragging my blue sack, I'd probably get away with it totally. Even my long hair hardly shows when I wear my *lunghi* (turban), but there are plenty of country people with long hair too.

It was obvious that the audience came from all levels of society. Some even had on smart western clothes. Men came and went, often with shawls hiding their faces—my friends said many were gangsters and murderers. One boy was pointed out to me as a fugitive, and I stole a look at him and thought he looked severely back at me. It was somewhat scary. My friends turned on, but I didn't because I felt strange enough in that weird atmosphere, and, much like on the steep hillside we had walked on, was afraid of falling off the roof which sloped slightly to the edge.

We sat on a mat near a brazier with tea brewing. A man wearing a white outfit walked around serving water to those who wanted it. My stomach felt none too good, possibly after the greasy lamb at dinner, but a lot of it had to be nerves. The music was probably the best to be heard in this country. Some phenomenally handsome and modern-looking boys were around, a few playing in the group around the old dervish. Music here, then, was the medium the dervish cult pursued, a religious thing like jazz, so the really hip people went for it. But you had to know it to understand it. I wonder if I'd dare go there alone?

We left after a time and walked back through impossibly dark and twisty alleys, dodging piles of shit, mud-holes, and garbage, to come back to the *khanega* of the Naqshbandi *dervishes*. I asked Abdul if it was dangerous to be out here at night and he said it used to be but wasn't anymore. I told him how dangerous streets of New York were.

Abdul's father had had to officiate at a wedding at the Bagh-e-Bala restaurant, earlier, and had only just returned, so we sat in the room of the little hunch-backed mullah waiting for the dervish meeting to start. A man outside on the balcony overlooking the courtyard was singing a long prayer. It was, by now, about midnight.

Soon we went into the main room where I had spoken with the old Dervish the week before. I was seated next to Abdul at the head of the room by his father, facing several curved rows of men seated on the floor a few feet away. People came and went. I saw one man who had been at the Chishti meeting. Though Abdul's friend, Mohammed, had said that all religions were welcome at dervish meetings, when I was asked earlier what my religion was I said Christian to make things easier. I couldn't break the bad news to them, though I also suspected they would probably not have minded that I was a Jew. Some of the men wore white embroidered skull caps, and there didn't seem to be any rule about head covering—some men were even bareheaded. My turban was satisfactory. The Chishti had a much hipper crowd than this, and larger, though many people crowded in here later on.

First, a supper was served, bowls of a brown, thick liquid with white gobs floating in it. It was to be a test of my soul and I had to drink it. It turned out to be hot chocolate and the white scum was curdled milk, about which I am especially sensitive. Bread was also served, so by eating bread with the chocolate I could avoid noticing the globs too much. Somehow I got it all down. But I could see that the men there loved it. Seconds were offered which I felt free to decline, though others accepted greedily. Then tea was served. How could they afford to feed all these people, I wonder?

Three or four soloists started singing, holding books that they used part of the time—I had the feeling it was a passion play they were telling, by the way people responded at times as though events were being related. These prayers were interrupted every half hour or so with everyone chanting the name of Allah, like the prayer the Dervish had taught me the week before, grunting a loud Hoo! hoarsely with the outward breath and gasping Allah on the inward breath, again and again, with swaying movements that got more violent as they gasped for breath, building in crescendo but keeping rhythm for the solo singer. Some of the men threw themselves so passionately into this chanting as though they could compel God to save them. It took a great effort to keep this up. One man spouted great gouts of saliva as he threw his head up and down, forcing himself. At first I was frightened by the giddiness I felt from the effort, so I held back and chanted in a modified way, for I felt I might faint or start screaming. Every time I thought I couldn't take anymore of this the Dervish sensed it and stopped us, and the soloists started again. Apparently he was controlling the order and pace of the religious exercise carefully.

There was no dervish dancing, as I'd been told, but I was hoping something like that would happen anyway. About 3:30 in the morning we all stood up and made a circle and the chanting got more intense and the prayers more fervent. I stopped watching the others and I too prayed for my soul, for help, for blessing. One man fell down and rolled around the floor in ecstasy, and I felt close to falling myself but held back. When the shaking and swaying and bowing reached a frenzy I thought surely some kind of whirling dance would take place, but it didn't. At the climax we were all standing in a circle, looking into our open palms shouting Al-LAH, Al-LAH in unison. I was trembling all over so much it was hard to hold out my hands, hard to stand up, while the old man's voice begged Allah to give us his blessings. One wild-looking creature who really had blown his mind and had rambled and mumbled and sometimes jumped about during the meeting, now wagged his head brokenly from side to side, seemingly beyond redemption.

Finally the Dervish said a closing prayer and we stood holding our open empty palms out, looking into them. The service was over. Some people kissed the Dervish's hand and I did too, gratefully, though I felt he might have been disappointed in me that I hadn't let go like the man who rolled around. Perhaps he had aimed the whole meeting at opening me up. I feel if I went again I would be purified, would give in to what had to work out of me. It was a marvelous prayer meeting and I'm still shaky from it, trembling.

But will I have the nerve to go again?

It was 4:30 and dawn. I waited in the Mullah's room while all the men said their morning prayers outside, which I as an outsider, regretfully, could not participate in, and then I walked home since there were no buses running yet. I was accompanied part way by another man who works with Abdul Mohammed on the Pactia Reclamation Project. He was a handsome man in a western way. He had offered me some opium early in the evening but I refused, not knowing what the night held, or how the opium would affect me. I noticed he had drowsed through the music. He explained opium to me. If it's hard, that means it's dirty. When boiled clean it becomes soft. I guess the piece I bought was dirty. It certainly tasted vile, like dung.

As we passed the police station where I got my visa renewed he said that he had been in jail there for three years for writing against the king. I think he said that they let him out weekends, but my Farsi was not up to getting all the details. I suggested to him that we put together a Farsi-English phrase book, which doesn't exist here. I could do the English side of it and he could do the Farsi.

He said that there were great forests in Pactia where monkeys lived, and that the people there were very dangerous. You had to go armed. He said he'd take me when he goes. He also said that he has family in Nuristan, and if I get permission to go he will give me a letter to them, but it isn't easy to get such permission. He himself is from Pashtoonistan, just over the border from Nuristan.

I asked him if he had ever been to the lakes at Band-i-ameer, but he hadn't, and when I praised them, he dismissed them as being for tourists.

As we walked back across town, my companion remarked how a year ago all this was bazaar with mud buildings, and now it was a row of modern buildings, mostly hotels, fronting the central park. Surely he meant five years ago. I said I thought they had too many hotels now for the few tourists, but he said the Pakistanis come and fill them up in summer to escape the heat there.

JULY 25. This morning I woke up feeling undone. To have to get up on such a day, not to speak of packing and going to a strange place, is unbearable.

The floor boys want *baksheesh*. There is no tipping really, but *baksheesh* is more like a gift. You could give anything. My floorboy still longs for my radio. Now he wants me to leave it with him while I'm in the north, but I know I'd never get it back. I know he's been playing it while I'm out because I found it not quite turned off. He's also eaten quite a few of my sugared almonds. I wonder if it was the sugared almonds that made me sick. There were a few bitter ones, as though some apricot seeds got mixed in. Perhaps I should give them to him so I don't eat them myself. What my stomach needs is warm milk for a few days, plain boiled rice or *kasha*, boiled potatoes, boiled chicken and broth, boiled beets. Maybe when I come back I should get a hot plate and a pot and a plate for the room. I could boil eggs too. I could even make my own yoghurt. I really can hardly eat the food here.

Luckily the bus to Kunduz does not leave from the outskirts of town and I'm able to take the city bus in front of the hotel directly to the bus terminal.

This bus to Kundoz isn't as bad as they usually are. There are a lot of cracked windows, true, but none are smashed. The seats are all numbered and reserved, but by the time children are squeezed in and bundles put in (no luggage racks and some things can't be entrusted to the roof) the bus will be overloaded and miserable. But the seats even have springs in them and so far no chairs have been set up for extra people in the aisle.

Dinny wrote asking me what Kabul looked liked and I can't describe it. The postcard views are all taken from above, from the surrounding hills, so you don't see the place from below with the hills behind it, which is the way it looks from down here. There's always a bare mountain with stone houses rising on it, almost blending into the rock except for dark squares of doors and windows. The mountains move nearer or farther according to the weather or time of day: the river that cuts through, roughly dividing old Kabul from new, is a stagnant series of dammed-up, scummy ponds where people bathe. I'll have to attempt the description of Kabul again sometime. At the moment it feels good to be out of it.

Kundoz. We rode over the Hindu Kush through the remarkable Salang Tunnel and, beyond it, through prosperous agricultural country, and arrived at 4:00 p.m. The government hotel in Kundoz is big and pleasantly ramshackle, set in its own garden. Bats are flying around the halls. I tried three bathrooms before finding a shower that worked well enough, but my room for 100 Afs. isn't bad. I wish these government hotels were cleaner though. Floors aren't ever cleaned, or hardly ever. Towels have to be asked for, and they're always gray and smelly. Sheets often have been slept in before—washed just means rinsed in cold water, and there are even hairs.

I met an American from California on the bus who is traveling with a knapsack. He walked to the hotel with me and has a room down the hall. He's a strange young man in his pink sweatshirt, baggy khaki pants, hiking boots, owlish glasses, and a big knapsack on his round shoulders. But he's so taciturn he makes me feel like a babbling fool. When he hoisted the knapsack onto his back, I remarked at how heavy it looked and he said it was the books. The books? I had an intuition and said I wished there was one book I'd brought with me, Gurdjieff's *Beelzebub's Tales to his Grandson*. He said that was one of the ones he had. So we got to talking and when I told him about my dervish experiences, he confessed to me he was going to look for a monastery in the mountains and was using Gurdjieff's book *Meetings With Remarkable Men* as a guidebook. He felt that if he had the courage to head into the mountains here—which would certainly be daring to do alone—he would be ready to find the monastery and the dervishes would come out to take him in. I had a fantasy that the Brotherhood in the mountains has a radar to spot Seekers like him and send out people to lead them astray.

When we got to the hotel I whipped out my introduction letter from the Tourist Office for the manager—with the American sitting there I felt like a pretentious fool. But it was the right thing to do, for there were no towels in our rooms and when I asked for them at the desk, amazingly, I was brought great bath towels as well as face towels, which was clearly the result of my magic letter—I have never gotten them anywhere else. I went with the *batcha* to bring them to the American, who was lying on his bed dully and made no response when I called out triumphantly that I'd gotten us towels. It didn't impress him in the least.

There was an Afghan artist on the bus who was going to his home in Badakshan above Faisabad for a month's vacation. He's a supervisor at the Teacher's College in Kabul and wants to sell his paintings in America. He's sold a lot to Americans here, scenes of Afghanistan. He wouldn't pay the price for a room at the government hotel, but went to a city hostel where a bed was 30 Afs. Yet he's flying to Faizabad. He was wearing western clothes, but says when he goes to America he will dress Afghani. I wonder.

Looking around, I see that Kundoz is a very lively country town, hot and dusty. The main street is paved and horse carriages go up and down. It seems to have industry. There's a regular whistle for the three shifts of the cotton factory. And there's quite a carpet bazaar. I looked at one shopkeeper's rugs and he had some good ones, but the one I wanted was priced at 8500 Afs. If I could get it for 2000 Afs., I'd take it. The hotel manager said he'd help me bargain. But what would I do with it if I got it? Lug it around until I got back to Kabul?

I tried to eat in what I was told was the town's best restaurant but couldn't get much of the greasy stuff down. I really can hardly eat the food here. As everywhere I've been, all the rice is flavored with the fat from the tail of the sheep—the local sheep grow a great lump of fat there. Perhaps I can live on bread, tomatoes, and fruit for a few days. Maybe eggs, if the hotel will cook them for me. But they told me they don't serve meals. What my poor stomach needs for a few days is plain boiled rice, boiled potatoes, boiled chicken and broth, boiled beets.

I came back early and took a shower. Without a shower this would be an impossible place, it's so hot and airless. I'll probably have to take several tonight. And I fear the little gnats will be getting me, for I've seen them in the lamplight.

The new governor is being installed today so the streets are being kept clean for the procession, and police are making everyone walk on the side. A party for the governor is going on in the garden, but in a far corner where I can't see it from my window. There is some kind of show being put on—I hear drums and music.

JULY 26. As I was leaving the hotel, I met an American glacierologist from the University of Minnesota who was part of an Austrian geological expedition in the Pamir mountains. I had met some of the party in Mazar. He's late in joining up with it because he got stomach trouble as soon as he arrived and was flying out today.

Kundoz is really quite a pleasant town and not as hot, it seems, as Mazar, but this morning a boy told me there's a lot of malaria here. I had breakfast at a tea house near the bus stop—I thought why pay 25 Afs. for tea and cold toast when I can have *nan* and tea in the village for 3-1/2 Afs. or less? The teahouse is decorated with gorgeous Indian movie posters, perhaps because it's next door to the movie house. Sitting on the rug-covered divan under some shady trees in front of the teahouse, I asked a very sexy carriage driver the words for fucking, cock, cunt, and balls in Farsi, and with great hilarity he told me. I was a little shy to ask further since quite a crowd gathered for the vocabulary lesson.

After breakfast I went to the rug bazaar and saw three or four rugs I liked, but nothing better than the one I saw yesterday, except for one old Bokhara that was quite worn but intricate, an antique. The man asked 10,000 Afs. for it, which is out of the question. A big, fat man who said he was a *kalantari* attached himself to me and took me around. I think this doesn't mean police but a notary, for he notarized a document in one place. It was no good going with him because he kept urging me to buy and I had to tell him quite sharply that I wasn't in a hurry. The man with the Bokhara said it would cost 50,000 Afs. ($600) in America, which is ridiculous. Another dealer gave me the price of a carpet in dollars, and I told him I had Afghanis and not dollars and walked out, for there's no dealing with him if he talks American prices. There are so few tourists here that they think of Americans as mythologically rich.

I saw some musical instruments hanging in a food shop and asked the man if there was a *khanega* of Chishti dervishes here and he said yes, to come to him at 6 o'clock Thursday evening and he'd take me, but I don't know if I can wait for that. Tomorrow is market day, which will be interesting, but what to do here after that? The hotel keeper says that without permission I can't visit Dasht-i-Archi, the village nearby that Zalmai recommended. Probably it's too near the Russian border. I bought six eggs from my Chishti dervish man who hard-boiled them for me.

I passed a man sitting in a tiny tea house with a baby parrot climbing on him. It was from Peshawar, he said. The bird seemed to know him and understand what he said, and liked especially clinging to his *lunghi*. Again I thought how strange that these people can communicate so well with animals.

Then in a *serail* I found a wrestling school where the arena is a small room open to the courtyard with a dirt floor, so the boys get covered with mud. The master did very complicated exercises to warm up. They were magnificently developed, and the mud matted their hair glamorously and defined their muscles. Then I walked away from town past the cotton mill and found another kind of sports club, just a room, where boys were lifting weights, making themselves ugly, in my view, and drinking milk out of a large aluminum vat that surely must have poisoned it.

At the far end of the main street past the paved part, there's a police barrier with an officer checking the identity papers of everyone coming into town from that direction. He called me over and I sat down with him. He said he had five children, but I knew from his eyes that he went for me. All these men I meet have women in their lives—mothers, wives, sisters, daughters. But I meet them on a level where women don't exist, except sometimes their young daughters may be allowed to come in.

I now think there's nothing more beautiful than a man wearing a white-on-white embroidered *peran* (shirt) and *tumban* (pants). It drapes the male torso to perfection.

Further on, through some dry, rattly woods I came to a country club with basketball, ping pong, and (alas) a bone-dry swimming pool. I was told that someone had drowned in it and it had been shut down. There was also a large athletic field where much melon eating was going on and a soccer game. In fact I have never seen so much melon selling, buying, and eating in my life as in this town. Everyone is carrying a melon. I get offered melon or tea everywhere. This clubhouse is built on a bluff where the land drops off into the river valley. There's a far view of green farmlands on the bottom and the Kundoz river winding through. The Soviet Union is not far away.

Walking back I met some boys, middle-class students, and they said at first they thought I was Afghan. I was pleased and think I can get away with going into areas forbidden to foreigners. I ought to try to get to the Amu Darya River on the Russian border.

I stopped in at the saddle and horse goods bazaar which also has a kind of woven pile-less rug. I saw a lovely old one and was asked 1600 Afs. for it, which perhaps would come down a lot if I stayed on here. This dealer is an Uzbek from Bokhara who was bitter about the Soviets because they were brutal trying to force the Muslims to drop their ancient ways. He gave me melon, and I bought from him a pair of brightly-knitted woolen stockings the *buzhkazi* riders wear under their boots. I'll wrap them and mail them from here to America.

JULY 28. I had a bad night and would like to stay in bed, but if I don't get up I can't see about mailing my package—a foolish quest, perhaps.

The trouble with this town ultimately is that there's nowhere cool to spend the day, no river teahouse to sit in, or fountain, or breezy hillside. Perhaps I should walk over to the Spinzar Country Club and see if there's any breeze and shade there.

The postmaster says this is the first time anyone has tried to send a "par-cel" to America from here, so they're in a quandary. But he's being quite good-natured about it. I first went to the customs chief who, after much palaver, wrote a note to the post office, personally guaranteeing that it contained only the *buzhkazi* stockings. I think one of the problems at the post office is that they don't know how much to charge me for the 400 grams it weighs. It should be about the same as the package I sent from Kabul, which was 50 Afs.

Headline in local paper: LOCAL POST OFFICE HANDLES PARCEL TO AMERICA. KUNDOZ MOVES AHEAD

12:30 PM. Failure. After all my efforts, the decision was No. I still could go to the governor and if he approved it, it would go through. But I haven't the nerve and the strength. It's just too hot. So I'm giving up. On my way back here from Faizabad I want to buy a number of things in the *buzkazhi* shops—long, long knitted scarves in natural color wool, weavings of various kinds, braided wool ropes, more *buzhkazi* stockings.

My itches are itching madly and I'm determined not to scratch. And my throat is really not good at all, so tomorrow if I can I'll get out of here. Faizabad should be cooler. But it seems so hard to get to I'm tempted to go back to Kabul. I keep thinking that it's not just the going, I'll have to do it all again on the way back. But perhaps it's easier coming back—I might even get a lift, or fly.

I walked to the town center and watched the traffic cops at work with their bullhorns—it must be a national campaign to make the streets less chaotic. There was only an occasional car or pedestrian or horse carriage, or a dog moseying across, but each got the full treatment: One cop indicated by waving his arms the route to take and the other instructed or admonished with the bullhorn. A pedestrian who tried to cut across was scolded loudly. Nobody jumped.

I bought bread, came back and paid my bill, and here I am alone in my room. I'm such a jerk, to be alone with a town full of handsome men out there. I wish I felt like studying Farsi but this place has taken the stuffing out of me. I don't dare relent and scratch even the worst bite because they seem connected and come alive even at the thought. I must stay firm. What is itching anyway? A form of pain? I long for my mail. I'm almost waiting till I can go home now. It feels like the summer is mostly over. But half-over is not mostly.

JULY 29. I'm in God's hands. I've set out for Faizabad. Leaving the hotel this morning, I walked to the far edge of town, what they call a "port," really a police control point, where one can find transportation for all towns in that direction, and took a truck over a bumpy road to another town called Khonabad where I was told I could get a jeep to Faizabad. Khonabad is a more interesting town than Kundoz and has a livelier bazaar, but the government favors Kundoz so Khonabad has rutted, dirt streets, and though only half an hour away, the world seems to have passed it by.

It turned out that there was no transportation directly to Faizabad from there either, so, racing me past what looked like fascinating shops, a little boy led me to the "port" on the other side of town where there was a truck going to Taluqan. I was assured that in Taluqan I could find a bus to Faizabad. It all sounded vague but I was moving in the right direction. I gave my little guide a 2Afs. coin, and it must have been plenty for his face lit up happily.

The "port" on the edge of town where I caught the truck to Taluqan was like a biblical scene, everything mud-colored—earth-brown shacks, flocks of sheep, goats, and donkeys, a stream where things were being washed, with not a tree or blade of grass.

The road went right through the stream, so our truck drove across, honking at the animals to get out of the way. Then we were in a lush river valley. On the bluff across from us over the river were flooded rice fields that spilled waterfalls down the banks.

It took over an hour to get to Taluqan—it was 10 a.m. by then. The bus to Faizabad was leaving at noon, and though everyone assured me it would arrive in Faizabad that night I didn't believe them—the bus was incredibly ramshackle and I could see it breaking down and stranding us in the desert. So I found a truck that was leaving immediately, climbed up the tailgate, and settled myself among a crowd of countrymen on top of rough bundles.

It was madness. The truck is impossibly crowded and uncomfortable and open to the sun. The road would be hard even to walk on—we bump over stones, ford rivers—we're way off the beaten track. We pass rice fields and cotton fields where there's irrigation. This hundred miles is going to take until tomorrow morning and has only begun. At every difficult or dangerous place in the road everyone strokes his beard and calls on Allah to help. In a long, stony riverbed where the truck was having difficulties, we all had to get out and walk. I thought, here I am, walking in the Hindu Kush.

The truck is not to be believed. It's decorated quite gaudily—psychedelic-style. I've seen them all over the place but this is the first time I've ever ridden on one. The truck, an old American cattle truck I guess, without a top but with the framework, is full of baggage and merchandise, often animals, and the people sit on top of it all as best they can, far too many of us. One relaxes into an easy mingling of knees and arms and legs. You lean where you can. It's a little like a hayride.

I noticed a rifleman was guarding us, riding on the front of the truck holding his rifle ready and was told there was danger here—Shuravi, the USSR—communist guerrillas, I think they mean. An old man showed me a cartridge belt he was wearing bandolier-style under his shirt. I couldn't figure out if he wanted to sell the ammunition to me or wanted to reassure me about the bandits. Some men have already tried out their pistols, aiming them, seemingly, at distant telephone wires. That could be why the phone line to Kabul was out yesterday when the postmaster tried to call for instructions about the parcel.

We've had to trudge over several more hills by now where the road was bad. Walking in a straggly column through the stony plain, mountains all around and far from everything I knew, I felt like it was a caravan, and now suppose I could manage that too.

We've stopped for a five-hour midday break at a way station and teahouse. We're in a valley with high mountains across from us—the Hindu Kush—with one great snowy peak. There are Kuchi tents and camels below, off by the river. I've had bread and tea and cucumber and am now lying in a field of alfalfa under a willow tree. There's a marvelous breeze blowing and it's pleasant except for the ants and spiders. Going through a village we brushed under the trees, which brought down on us a shower of bugs, ticks and ants and spiders.

I had the itchiest time last night in Kundoz. I woke up and my bites were shrieking to be scratched. The trouble is even brushing them with the towel or sheet makes them shriek louder.

My fellow passengers aren't too friendly. They question me closely and seem annoyed by my inability to understand much of what they say. I should have answered that I was married when they asked, for they seemed astonished and contemptuous to hear that I'm not. One man said he had two wives and another three. Fifteen, sixteen seems to be the age girls get married. When I said some girls in America get married at twenty-five, they looked amazed that anyone would want such an old woman. Some resent me wearing my *lunghi*, but it's the best protection against the sun, and one end of it can be wrapped around the face against the dust. One man wanted to trade knives with me and was angry when I wouldn't. My writing also turns them off. In general I'm getting a hostile reception, but often the day after I turn on I notice this. Perhaps my fear of people is brought out by the hashish and affects my relations with them.

Everyone seems very curious about what I have in my bags. They feel them and try to peer in and ask what's in there. It's almost more than curiosity and I wonder what will happen. They ask for various items of my clothes as gifts (*baksheesh*), my watch, my *lunghi*. I may give the boy who helps the driver my blue socks. They also like to compare my knife and wristwatch with theirs. Since I can read the roman letters, they asked me to read the inscriptions on their watch dials. But my eyes are no longer good enough for such small print and the truck's jiggling makes it hard to focus. Their watches are often Russian-made, with 16 or 24 jewels and I try to explain that their Russian watches are much more valuable than my jewel-less Timex, and a trade wouldn't be fair to them. What makes my wristwatch so desirable, I think, is the silvery, expandable band.

They say that the truck was made in America and is a very good one, that Russian motors are no good. But when I point out that all the drivers say the Volga is the best car for Afghan roads, they agree. I always avoid mentioning the jeeps which are mostly Russian here. (I did see a Willys jeep today.) The name jeep being American would only confuse the issue.

We actually have a woman on board who has sat nearly silent in her veil the whole time. She never gets off at the rest stops either. I pity her.

The truck is now stopped in a river gulch and is standing in the water. We've bumped our way to here and have a million bumps ahead.

Things are better now. I'm becoming by degrees a guest, and that means being treated well if not warmly. Still, some of the people are becoming friendlier. I've decided the men aren't hostile to me, except for a few psychotics who are poisoning the atmosphere. By me, if one person doesn't love me, everybody hates me.

Halfway, we passed through the town of Keshem, set in a lush valley, an extremely attractive place. The people were really darling and super-friendly. We stopped at a teashop and I immediately made friends it was hard to tear myself away from. I was tempted to get off the bus and stay. The name of the town, Keshem, derives from Kush, as in the Hindu Kush mountains. These are the mountains that might hold the secrets of Gurdjieff.

I'm now being urged to evening prayers. A young man wants to instruct me in the procedure. First you pee, carefully wiping the last drop off with a leaf. Then you wash your hands, mouth, face, ears, and nose, blowing it carefully, then the feet. The water is unfortunately too dirty from the irrigation ditch or I'd make the attempt. A marvelous river is running noisily further below and I wish I could throw myself into it, but it's too far. Happily, the rigors of the trip have calmed the itching of my bites somewhat. It's beautiful how the men are lined up, praying into the last rays of the sun and one star risen above it. The mountains stand about us, bare and deserted-looking, but of course they're not deserted. There are always people in the landscape.

Our road has been along the channel of the river. I kept wanting to throw myself in. But the trip itself has been a kind of baptism. For I see there is nothing to fear on any trip in Afghanistan. Everybody looks cutthroat— there are more one-eyed men here than anywhere, I expect. The one bad eye usually has a white iris as though it were boiled. Even difficult people, as these certainly are, can be faced. And if it's uncomfortable it's also fascinating. Nobody speaks a word of English but the driver's helper has really worked to make me understand the language.

Even after dark the truck maneuvered over the most dangerous roads, crawling on one mountain track with a rushing stream far below, with frequent calls to Allah from the passengers. We passed a Kuchi nomad camp and we could see all the camels sitting on the ground and among them groups of people, some with cooking fires lit.

And now my fears have come true. We've stopped for the night at a restaurant/tea house where we are going to sleep over. Along with most of the men, I'm settled on a straw mat spread over the dirt along the front of the low stone building, feeling hot, sticky, itchy, and exhausted. There's a storm lantern hung overhead so I can write. It would be quite pleasant here under the trees if I could shower and had some bedding and a leopard coil to keep away bugs. I don't even have a blanket. Everyone is shocked that I'm not eating the food, just bread and tea. They urge me to eat the *palau*, but I'm not taking any chances.

I was asked to sing, since I claim to be a poet, a *shah-er*, and I gave a miserable performance of a Greek song, that I thought they might respond to, but I was really too tired.

We're supposed to get into Faizabad at eight in the morning. That means leaving at dawn. I've noticed that it's not considered important to tell me the exact truth about time and place and arrival. I heard one man say, after he had said we'd ride all night, that it didn't make any difference what they told me.

I took some charcoal pills before starting out this morning to ward off any tendency to diarrhea. I hope and pray the inhibiting force is great enough to carry through the trip. I'm not even sure I can shit wearing these baggy Afghani drawers, for when I drop them they fall into a great wide heap and I have to hold them gathered in one hand. Having to wash your ass afterwards without getting the clothes wet is no easy trick, especially with only one free hand. How these people manage I'll never understand. Yet their drawers never get wet or stained. The only thing that smells about them is their feet.

These clothes are best worn in a breeze—to feel all that flimsy cloth rippling about one's naked body is one of the supreme pleasures. I can understand women who prefer gauzy and ruffly clothes.

Water in cool silver tumblers is being brought around by the host, but I dare not drink. I wonder if I could get a bottle or pitcher of drinking water and drop some water-purifier pills into it. Do I dare open my suitcase and take out my toilet kit? I know that everything I own would be coveted. If they were the *doshman* (the bandits or enemy) they all keep talking about, they'd strip me clean. The only difference between them and the *doshman* is that these men are on the bus and the doshman is lurking along our route. They could easily switch roles.

I refused the offer of sleeping on the divans of the teahouse with their woolen rugs, for outside here it seems less buggy, but I'm under the light and the insect life is elaborate and vast. I'm itchy but must resist scratching. I must not suffer. Reject the insect problem once and for all. I can be strong-minded up to a point.

I watched the men laying out their bedding. Some of the bedrolls are quite elaborate: a rug first is laid down, then a mattress, a cloth for a sheet, and then blankets or quilts and a pillow. One passenger has a satin patchwork comforter and in general his bedding is too fancy for the occasion. Several of the men, after whispering together, sneaked off into the dark beyond the teahouse to sleep. Were they making dates?

I was addressed as taka (uncle), which is a big improvement over "mistáh." I had explained to one boy that I didn't like to be called Mistáh and for friends it was inappropriate. People are also addressed as *batcha* (boy) or *baba* (papa), so I guess I fall in-between, in the uncle class. A boy is going around collecting some money for sleeping there and addressing everybody as *kaka*. But he hasn't asked me. I'm a guest.

A procession of men riding donkeys passes by. The men do not turn their heads. A baby donkey as usual follows. There's always a baby camel, or a colt, following the riders. The dogs bark as they pass, those frightening dogs with cut-off ears and tails. They say if you sit down they won't attack.

Here I am, lying in front of a tea house under sycamore trees on a woven mat on the clayey ground, my sack and *lunghi* for a pillow, my jacket under me, a high-powered gas lamp over the door, with men on divans talking or sleeping. I lie down where I am and get up in the morning. I don't make demands on life. I think the message for today is to go without fear, that Allah will provide. Am I learning?

JULY 30. Dawn. The lights went out last night at 11:00 P.M. But I hardly slept. The dogs barked madly, doing their job of protecting the property. And they had a lot of work to do, for camel trains kept passing all night in the starlight. It was very glamorous to see parading against the sky the beautiful nomad women on the camels' backs, draped with all their heavy jewelry, the nomad men dashing about on white stallions.

It got chilly toward morning and my cotton jacket wasn't enough. The man sleeping next to me, a handsome soccer player, kept one foot on mine all night. Once he tugged at my pants to pull me toward him.

The *serail* keeper wouldn't take money from me this morning so I realized again that I was a guest. After tea we piled back into the truck. The vast valley was stunning, but the road minimal, clinging to the mountainside above a gorge, almost falling into the river. Luckily there was no traffic, for two cars couldn't have passed. The truck barely inched by overhanging rocks. There was about four hours of that.

The men talked a lot about *doshman* and when I asked who the enemy was they said *shuravi*, which is the USSR in Farsi.

We arrived in Faizabad about 11:00 A.M. The hotel is a worse dump than usual. It's called the Mayor's Club (pronounced Ka-loob), and is the only hotel available to foreigners— 50 Afs. a night. When I asked about the pretty little hotel clinging to a rock in the river, the very hotel that I saw the picture of in the National Geographic magazine story on Afghanistan in the dentist's office, they said it was closed and was only for official government guests. I suggested I might qualify as an official guest but was told it was empty of furniture. I'm disappointed but I guess the Ka-loob is where I have to stay. Nothing is going to be easy here. And the hotel man-of-all-work, the *batcha*, is sullen and immovable. When I asked for the manager, hoping for better treatment, I was told he got married yesterday and is away on his honeymoon, so nothing is possible. Actually, the room could be nice if it were better furnished. It has two battered chairs, a filthy carpet, and the bed is a sagging wreck, with dirty sheets and a lumpy gray pillow. The table also leans perilously. There's a toilet yes, though it's only a filthy hole. There's even a wash room—but no towels or mirror or running water, just a large water tank that turned out to be empty. And when I asked for water the boy said I should go wash in the river.

Our arrival in Faizabad was inauspicious. Because of police problems, the driver said, we had to get out of the bus at a serial well short of the town and walk in across the high bridge over the river—it was a hot walk. The town is the real thing, though, and worth coming to, with nothing beyond it but the Soviet Union in one direction and the Pamir mountains and China in the other. No wonder it's a sensitive area. From the serail where our truck pulled in and unloaded us and the freight, I was followed to the hotel by a soldier and when I got there I learned I had to go with him to the police commissioner immediately, for he said I needed permission to stay here. It was another exhausting, hot, long walk through the endless main street of the bazaar that follows the hilly landscape up and down. The little soldier was pleasant, but I had to lug my own bag with me because apparently it's not safe to leave it in the hotel.

I went from one official to another, each of whom put on an intimidating act of scowling. At first it was, What are you doing here? But when I showed them my letter from the tourist office they changed their tune, and I was invited to stay as long as I liked, go to Baharak and Jurm (towns further up the valley), eat melon—oh yes, and teach one of them English. Perhaps if I'd arrived by plane my reception would have been pleasanter. As it was, I had an hour of police formalities. It's good for my Farsi, at least.

After the melon, the little soldier was assigned to take me to the hotel, though not to carry my bag. I noticed the shops had all the buzhkazi stuff I liked in Kundoz. I must see if things are cheaper here. I could take a lot of it back with me. I know one thing, I'm flying out of here. I couldn't make that overland trip twice.

At the hotel, without the manager, there was no room for me at first, then a room at the back, then this one on the river side, but still uncomfortable and dirty. I'll spray it before going out. I guess I have no choice but to go to the river and bathe and wash my clothes.

I want to make some friends here, besides all those police officers who give me the wim-wams. The soldiers kept coming in and saluting with heel clicks, like fascists. Even civilians stand smartly and salute. There's an atmosphere of brutality and ruthlessness. The police said they would come visit me at the hotel. I hope they come immediately and scare the hotel people into being nicer to me.

I see that opening the window was a mistake. All the flies came in.

JULY 31. There's a young French couple staying here also, and I suggested that we walk over to the government guesthouse and see if it's really closed, as I was told. We walked out to it over a short stone causeway bridging one channel of the river to where it's perched on its rock, just like the picture, and found it empty and locked up, but in a few minutes an old man showed up and unlocked it for us. It's much nicer than the Ka-loob, and he said we could stay there. There are two buildings, a main house with four tiny, single bedrooms around a large living/dining room, and a small annex clinging to the rock around which the torrent swirls, and which has a single bedroom and a double. These rooms open right onto the rushing water of the stream, facing up the valley toward the high Pamirs and China.

I'd like the single room in the annex. I've told the man I'm moving in this morning. It costs 100 Afs. a person, which is twice what the Ka-loob costs, but is really beautiful and clean, and worth it. There must be a conspiracy to keep it empty. I suppose most tourists automatically are fed to the other hotel, the Ka-loob.

As I walked out of the hotel to wash my clothes at the river, a young man of unpleasant appearance followed me everywhere, even though I tried to shake him. When I finally confronted him and asked him why wouldn't he go away he said he was police. So I said I had my permission from the police to stay and walked angrily off. He was gone when I looked around again. It was my first experience in being tailed, except for the soldier who followed me from the truck serail to the hotel, but he was in uniform. This one was plain-clothes.

At the river I washed my clothes as best I could, laying them out on the stones to dry, trying to avoid the shit everywhere along the bank. I attracted a small crowd of very mean kids who started demanding various items of clothes. I felt any minute they would get together and start pulling me apart. One little boy actually threw a stone at me and ran away. Then all the others threw stones at him and I couldn't stop them. I very cautiously took a swim near to the shore, for the river seems terribly dangerous. I must find a better place to bathe, perhaps further upstream. But I'm afraid of the Kuchi nomads' dogs—this area is an important Kuchi summer campground. People keep saying that the dogs won't attack if you sit down. But what if it didn't work?

The children urged me to go further out into the river, but it was obviously dangerous and they would have had a good laugh at my expense. Or perhaps that is my paranoia which is in full sway here. A man working at a supply shed by the hotel told me that a boy was seized by a large fish last week and drowned. As we were talking we saw a boy bathing naked across the river and the man started throwing rocks at him, but luckily the boy was too far. I sense this kind of viciousness everywhere here. The way the police dominate the town has increased the evil in the people. Perhaps they were always dangerous in this remote border area. If I stop for anything, it attracts a crowd and people aren't friendly. Many of the townspeople also seemed hostile to me yesterday and spit when I passed. But I'd had no sleep and thought maybe my vibes were bad. As I become known I'm hoping things will warm up.

I asked several people about a *khanega* and actually found a man who told me of one in Jurm and one nearby, but I was too tired last night to try to go.

There are also two American boys from California at the Ka-loob who stay in their room a lot, being sick and perhaps permanently stoned. They never got the big police treatment I had, but they've been taken several times to a small police station at this end of town. They drove here in their own car, which I suppose makes them more invisible, or puts them in the upper class, wrecky though the car is. The French couple came by plane and haven't been bothered at all, although last evening they walked over to the police station to ask permission to stay. Admittedly, I am a more suspicious-looking character than the others. In Kabul the Tourist Office says tourists are free to come here, but the police have their own ideas and intend to keep control— with the borders of the USSR and China nearby, they're suffering from the usual military paranoia.

There are some vehicles parked in the lot by the hotel from some expedition that is off in the mountains. But the two Americans and the French couple and I are the only tourists here. The Americans hardly go out except for food. They said they drove to the snow, which was very far. But their car battery is now dead. They say they're very weak. From the poor diet? From illness? Perhaps from staying stoned. On what, I wonder? Maybe opium.

My first impression on waking up this morning in the Ka-loob was that the mountainside across from me and the river valley looked like a desert. The rushing water hardly sounds like water. A fountain is more watery than this torrent. The road runs along the other bank of the river and camel trains of Kuchis were going by loaded with tents, felt mats, and wives.

I'll go have tea and *nan* and then move to the other hotel.

Breakfast at the tea house became a public assembly with the truck driver's young assistant telling everyone all about me. *Shah-er* (poet) seems to be a very respected occupation here and the word is said with reverence. On the truck when he'd asked me about my salary, I foolishly explained I had none and made my living giving lectures at colleges and earned from seventy-five to one hundred dollars for each, which is not the truth, but the reality of my fees would be incredible to him so I cut them way down.

I should have made my fee even lower, for it sounds unbelievable to these people. I also shouldn't have said I was unmarried. This seems to have gone around the town because yesterday as I passed a shop one man turned to the other and said, "He has no wife." I also heard one man saying something to the effect that I wasn't a Muslim so I was worthless. That may be why some of the men spit as I pass. It is of course a pretty small town.

My bread and tea cost 1-1/2 Afs.

The truck I arrived on was about to return to Taluqan and the driver again asked for my knife. I politely refused, pointing out he had a knife and I needed mine. He's a very handsome man and I hated to turn him down. The truck people aren't warm in manner—nobody will look you deep in the eyes and they don't hold hands or put a hand to the heart on parting. Yet they're good people. I prefer more openly sentimental people.

Yesterday when the French couple set off for the police station everyone at the hotel said no one would be there at that hour, but today I spoke with them and they had no trouble getting permission to stay and to go to Jurm as well. Was my experience there unusual? Today I have a tail again, a charming young soldier from the town of Keshem where the truck stopped. I might as well be friends with him.

I've packed and left the *Ka-loob*. The torn 50 Afs. note I gave the *batcha* for my room was returned with the implication it was no good. So I gave him a newer bill and came here to the guesthouse where the old man gave me a room. Now I'm all alone in the little house on a rock in the middle of the turbulent river that I fell in love with when I saw it in the National Geographic. The walls are white and clean with a straw-mat ceiling and clean, hand-woven rugs on the floor. There's even an electric light. The room is simply furnished with a bed, a table, a bench, and curtained French windows overlooking the rushing waters. It's almost perilous.

The bathroom here is as simple as can be, a little room with a low ledge around it and at the end a hole for shitting and peeing, and on the ledge to one side a spigot with a large can of water and a mug for dipping water out. I wonder if one pushes the shit down the hole with the twig broom. Or aim precisely. This elementary bathroom can only be used if you do everything in the squatting position. It's like morning exercises. I'm sure my legs will be in better shape from it.

It's nice to be here, but though perfect, also lonely. Well, I'll bring in food, and if the old man will give me a bottle of water and a glass, I'll be all right. I got what I wanted—I moved in here, to the picture in the National Geographic—and now I realize that in the other place, the Ka-loob, there were people at least. It's what happened at home when I was fourteen and finally got my own room after campaigning for it: I shut the door and was miserable. I really am on a bummer here. Flee back to Kabul? But I'm too tired after that trek to go anywhere.

The French couple also wanted to move in but the old man insisted on charging them for two beds even if they took a room with one. They argued that a room with a single bed should be 100 Afs., even if two people sleep in it. But he said no, 200 Afs. was the price for two people. They're going to Jurm today and I wish I could go with them, but the Commandant asked me to come to him first if I wanted to go to Jurm.

Yesterday I was talking with some of the truck people in the serail when a jeep of the Ministry of Agriculture came by, and an official got out and said, "Mistah, what do you want?" My first reaction was a feeling of offense and I said, "What do you want?" He repeated his question so I said, "Nothing." He then asked if I was a tourist and invited me to take a drive with him, but I was too tired and refused. This question, What do you want? or Where are you going? sounds very aggressive to me, but I have to remind myself that they might think I need something if I look into a shop or talk to strangers. And they always assume a tourist is passing through on his way to somewhere else. This is not called the Crossroads of the World for nothing.

The old caretaker has come into my room and seems to be looking around surreptitiously and is giving me the creeps. Has he been asked by the police to spy on me? I sent him out for a bottle of water and a glass.

My new Afghani outfit has shrunk an incredible amount and is quite trim now. I wouldn't have thought that cold water would have shrunk the cotton so much. I wonder if the origin of knickers isn't from outgrown *tumbans*, these baggy pants they wear here that gather at the ankles, I see boys wearing *tumbans* they have outgrown which reach only below the knees and they look like knickers. And at home only boys wear knickers.

The flies are being pesky and I guess that is a permanent problem if you open the window during the day. Amazingly, I just sprayed one of them and he went away, never to return, I hope. The room now smells of it though. I hope it doesn't poison me. For the moment at least, amazingly, there are no more flies.

The old man is back and is telling me he hasn't taken a wife because he has no money to buy one. A wife costs 40,000 Afs. here. He says he's from Jurm. I'm trying to get rid of him by asking what he wants, where his room is, with no success. He wants something I'm sure. He's been looking toward my bags longingly. I'll give him my socks as *baksheesh*.

I think I understand: The old man (and he is not really old) just said he was going to the bazaar, so I think he considers himself at my service. Perhaps he will do some simple cooking for me. And I'm sure he would shop for me.

This room is extraordinarily beautiful. I think it's positioned to escape the sun, for now hardly a ray seems to come in and the sun will set on the other side.

One thing I could do to make myself less noticeable would be to get a sack instead of a valise. My fat suitcase, small as it is, has been arousing curiosity everywhere, for what could be in it? No one would believe I needed all those things. And for here I don't—I can live with one change of clothes. I could leave the suitcase at the Tourist Hotel in Kabul and just carry necessary things in a sack of some kind. But a sack is so porous everything would get filthy.

The old man just went out to the market and he'll tell everyone about me. I suppose I could have asked him to shop for me. But what else have I got to do?

I'd like to follow the tributary of the river that goes through the town, cutting it in half. If I could get to the source it might be a good place to wash and drink.

My resolution not to scratch my bites was a wise one. I still itch but I have fewer scabs and it seems to me that I itch less. There are as many bites though and I wonder if I'm getting new ones. Perhaps fleas will be a problem here. I'll spray the room when I go out.

One question I don't understand: I'm often asked, Is Afghanistan good or is America good? As if I'm supposed to choose between them.

I'd like to leave Afghanistan immediately. Life is too hard. I miss Europe, with its good food and cities of comfort. So orderly and civil and clean. I'd like to be in London. It feels like I'll never get out of here alive. This place especially frightens me.

The mystery is solved: The governor is coming here for a picnic tonight. So I was seen to be in the way. But he's only going to be at the main house. There could be a police guard to keep everyone out and me in.

I went out and bought a melon and bread, for I may be stuck here tonight. I'm very hungry but not for melon or bread. I'd hoped to get some eggs, but I ran into all the policemen from the headquarters in civilian dress, and the one who wanted to learn English clung to me, and I had to plead a bad stomach, so I got away. He threatens to come by tomorrow for an English lesson. There was also the possibility of finding *mast* (yoghurt), but I had to turn back to escape him. The Police Chief got his official appointment yesterday so there were many congratulations. He's the most attractive of the lot. He looks plump and Jewish.

We spoke of religion and when they asked me about mine I said Christian. I was surprised to learn that in Afghanistan there are few Shiites but mostly Sunnis, who don't follow Ali. Yet Ali's tomb is in Mazar and everyone there seemed to revere it.

I'm sitting by my window in the late light. Soon it will be dark and I fear the electric light won't go on, for it depends on someone getting the town generator going. That wouldn't be a disaster, except that this evening with the governor's picnic being prepared outside—they're preparing hundreds of kabobs and buckets of palau and salad, I heard—I don't feel free to come and go. I must go out for tea, though. Maybe the *batcha* will bring me some.

The police this evening said foreigners weren't allowed to stay in this hotel. I don't believe it: Everyone says anything they want to. But perhaps one should arrange to stay here in advance, before leaving Kabul.

A young town official who lives in the other hotel and has his office there—something to do with public utilities—came by with a friend to visit me this afternoon. Everyone seems free to walk right in and sit down. The friend was really charming, a school teacher, who unfortunately goes in for body building. He told me his heart was "hot." Yes, it is hot—I felt it. He had such beautiful, open, dark eyes. I invited him to come back—profusely—but he was vague.

Miracle of miracles, the light works and it's a hundred-watt bulb, enough to read by—if I had a book.

AUGUST 1. I woke up this morning in this incredible room, the cold river air pouring in, the sound of the torrent smashing about me. It's a room one must stay in. There really is nothing in town compared to this.

Last night the nice man knocked on the door and invited me to come down and eat the good food of the picnic, but I couldn't. I was too shy. I would have been presented to the governor, surely. It was rude, I know, for he assured me I was a guest. The rules of being a guest are strict and you don't say no. I wonder who this man is? He seems truly kind.

I was so homesick last night, I panicked, afraid that I was a prisoner here. The police chief acts nice to me but I know he's capable of anything and has done what was necessary to get to his position. He is a really dangerous man. This is the furthest point of my trip and I felt the hopelessness of having reached it. I could only think of Europe and home. But what have I to do with those cities of Europe? After this, how boring the museums are, and even the restaurants and cafes and movies. But still, in imagination, the cities seem gorgeous, with their green parks and handsome buildings. And loved ones not far away. I don't long for America, except perhaps San Francisco. I'm thinking of Rome, Paris, Amsterdam, London, and—I'm ashamed to say it, but I will—civilization. August in Paris is so beautiful.

What is it I most long for here? Just the fountain in Kabul.

I keep thinking of how to go to the airport, where to buy the ticket. But I know I'll regret leaving, if I flee. I'm in that photograph in the National Geographic, the very hotel in the river. I can't leave now. Maybe I'm still tired from the trip. I'll just stay put. I feel my bites will mostly subside here. A lot of the old scabs from Mazar have fallen off. I've got a few new ones though. I suspect the pillow is a haven for fleas.

I feel better about the village. I went through the bazaar and met the charming cross-eyed boy who led me to a shop where he repairs shoes, where we sat. I helped him with his English and he helped me with my Farsi. Also on the street I met the weight lifter and he kissed me— he's an angel.

I mailed some letters from the post office and walked up into the hills behind the village. I was wary, but lots of people were friendly. What I did was follow the water ditches upward, hoping to come to the source, but so cleverly are the aqueducts built that the water comes from far away around the mountains and sometimes even seems to run uphill. This must be an illusion. There are even tunnels in places. I feel that if I could find a source, a spring, I could drink and be refreshed. Water down here doesn't satisfy.

I find it remarkable that there are absolutely no women visible in the bazaar, just some little girls. I saw a few women at a distance among the houses when I was above the town, but apparently they're almost completely secluded.

My sore throat from Kundoz where it turned into laryngitis seems to have turned into a cold and I'm blowing my nose a lot. The dust of the trip did it no good and last night I foolishly left the window and even the drape open, so the cold river wind blew on me all night long. But it was delicious.

I bought two very soft, very long, knitted scarves, one for 120 Afs. and the other for 100 Afs. I must buy more of these beautiful scarves, and perhaps the rough wool bags that can be used for rugs by opening them up. There are many useful items for horses and donkeys that are decorated beautifully. But I guess they're useless to me. But I love the braided wool ropes.

I also bought three eggs which the *batcha* is cooking for me. I gave him my blue socks as baksheesh. The eggs were priced at 2 Afs. each and though I argued the boy refused to sell them for less. But when I bought two, the *sahib* showed up and gave me an extra one for *baksheesh*. I suspect I'm bargaining too hard here.

I see if I don't lock my door people feel free to just come in and sit down. The *batcha* from the Ka-loob is here now with my *batcha*, so I have two fairly filthy guests . My *batcha* has brought in tea, which is terrible, and they keep staying.

The French couple have come back from Jurm, the *batcha* from the Ka-loob said. I must call on them this afternoon.

After we finished tea, they left, but the batcha from the Ka-loob was so dirty he left a dark stain on the carpet where he sat. Could it be I'm free of them for awhile? Now if I could just get rid of the flies. I'm a little afraid of the Japanese aerosol spray. It could be dangerous for me as well as for the flies. Nobody tries to do a thing about flies here. They don't even brush them away or anything. Perhaps it is hopeless, but I'm sure it could be dealt with over the years. I like to plan imaginary national campaigns against flies. It would be so good not to have bites. I always seem to have new ones. From where?

I wish I could go swimming, but where to avoid the onlookers and especially the children who seem absolutely rapacious. I think I'm allergic to boys of 8 through 14, the most dangerous age—they're capable of anything.

They really don't use special words for breakfast, lunch, or dinner, like the grammar says. The word is always the same—it's simply bread, *nan*. Do you want to eat bread? *Nan merkhouri*? But that nan could mean *palau* or *khorma* (stew) as well.

I still have the feeling about Afghanistan that it's possible to wake up one morning and be very happy. But it hasn't happened yet.

This is like living in a mill house with the waterfall going over it. Or living in a perpetual storm with the trees being rocked and tormented. The waters are my tormented spirit, the storm of my loneliness. I should have invited the cross-eyed boy to come tonight at sunset to sit in my window as the darkness falls.

I asked who the nice man was who let me stay here yesterday and invited me to the picnic. He is the *ashpaz*—the cook—which here is more like the major *domo*. But whose *ashpaz* I don't know. He reminded me a little of Gul Baz, Rosamond Klass's manservant, whom she writes about in *Land of the High Flags*, her book on Afghanistan that I read avidly. [It has recently been reissued by Odyssey Books (2007)]

This place is enchanted—this room I mean. It is one of the most beautiful places I have ever stayed. There was the luxurious Mamounia Hotel in Marrakesh with the palm grove below and a view of the snow-capped peaks of the High Atlas mountains in the distance—and with the ludicrous out-of-season price of $10 a night that included wonderful bathrobes, both in the room and at the pool. And another, far more simple room on the harbor at St. Tropez, where Neil and I debated whether to spend the $7 it cost.

There was just a knock on my door (which I bolted, though it isn't done), and I was sure it was the man from the police who wants English lessons, so I didn't answer. But suppose it was one of my young friends or the French couple? I think I'll walk over to the Ka-loob and see the French couple if they are in. While I'm out, I must also try to find the bank—I only have notes of 500 Afs., which are too large for anyone to change.

I wonder if I could catch some fish in the river and get the restaurant to grill them on kabob spits? Maybe there are fish hooks for sale. But in this wild water where would you drop a line?

I went to the bazaar and bought another scarf for 100 Afs. Another even prettier was offered to me for 70 Afs. but it felt a little prickly.

I ran into the French couple bargaining hard for high boots, and then the cross-eyed boy who walked me through the bazaar. But when we passed the police station and were walking by an athletic field near a barracks, perfectly harmless, it seems to me, the soldier who tailed me the first day called out and severely reprimanded me for going where I shouldn't have gone. The Commandant was out in front of the police station so I went up to him and apologized for my mistake, for I felt the little soldier was only acting tough to impress his boss. When I said goodbye, I turned and saluted ironically in the little soldier's direction. The odd thing is he had been following the French couple when I met them, and he must have switched to following me when I passed, without my noticing. It's more and more clear to me that this is a military outpost on a sensitive border.

When the soldier called out, my young companion hurriedly stooped to wash himself in an irrigation ditch and said he had to go to the mosque to pray. I hope he didn't get into trouble, but he had said that this was a public garden or park, so who knew it was off limits? It must have been a close call for him, because I'm sure the soldiers would have been brutal, if he did anything wrong.

I bought apples from Jurm, 4 Afs., and, extravagantly, a bottle of Russian mineral water the French couple recommended. But I noticed several partly-filled bottles on a table and think they were manufacturing it, for the bottle leaked when I put it upside down in my sack and when I tasted it, it had a strong taste of iodine. Yet the cap was hard to remove.

The French couple only got as far as Baharak by nine last night, so they gave up on Jurm and came back today. There was a bridge out on the road and their truck driver refused to cross the makeshift one. Then they caught another truck but it kept breaking down all the way. The road is really dangerous. A jeep fell off and two men were killed today. I don't think I'll risk it.

The French couple paid 35 Afs. for the same knitted stockings I got in Kundoz for 70 Afs. And theirs were prettier. I want to buy a few more pairs of them. And a striped wool sack. I also saw a little prayer rug today for 1200 Afs. at the rug shop in the bazaar. The local people do have a sense of tourist prices and usually hold to their price.

They told me the American boys at the Ka-loob were very sick with dysentery. Maybe I should go try to help them. The *batcha* there is really useless.

With the French couple, I met the young official who lives in the Ka-loob along with his weightlifter friend, who didn't kiss me this time—I think the presence of a woman inhibited him. Then we all continued on together down the street and I noticed he held hands with his friend. They must be lovers. The weight lifter's father is Minister of Education in this province, so he's been here a long time. He has a small room that he works out alone in, but in Kabul he and his friends work out together. The young official is from Kabul and hates it here. Everyone assigned by the government to managerial jobs in the provinces hates where they are, like the staffs of the government hotels. If local people were appointed, everything would be run better.

The French couple are leaving in the morning. Now why didn't I invite them here tonight? We could have shared the melon. The plane leaves at noon but it will be a slow trip to the airport by truck so they must start early. I said I'd come by the Ka-loob to see them off.

The children are getting really fresh, imitating my strange speech. One of them offered me a teenage boy passing by. Which reminded me that in Kundoz at the teahouse where I usually had breakfast, one of the buggy drivers, a really husky, handsome man, offered me a teenage boy sitting next to him, stroking his cheek and telling be how soft and smooth he was. I said he was *shirin*, sweet, and the remark seemed to be acceptable.

Some men told me a wife here costs 20,000 Afs. and up. You're limited to four wives however.

The light is still on at 10:40 though the *batcha* said it would go off at 10:00. Marvel that it is, the light has unfortunately attracted some flying insects and I fear for myself tonight. I feel all bitten up again. I've been scratching again a little, and must remember my vow—to decide firmly not to scratch, once and for all. Accept the itching. I just got up and sprinkled the mattress and pillow with DDT. My itching is tormenting me again and I can't sleep. I see a lot of tiny black gnats on the white sheet. I'd better cover up or get eaten alive.

AUGUST 2. I'm wild to leave this town, and to leave Afghanistan. Is it that I just want to keep moving? I awoke with a strange dream of being a slave. There were numbers of slaves/prisoners and when guards passed they could make them perform whatever indecencies they wanted. A girl and boy were crying hysterically. I escaped by going through a wooden building. I heard the Commandant say, "What do these people want?"

I'll be glad to get out of here. Today I must go to the airline office. Find something to make a package with, maybe buy a sack to wrap my things in. I see myself spending a last week in Kabul and then leaving for Herat and the border.

I've decided that those little gnats were fleas. How fragile they are. You wipe them and they're a black stain on the sheet. Could I have brought them into the room with the scarves? I should have sprayed them immediately.

I couldn't sleep last night for a long time, excited by the thought of moving on. I can' t stay in one place, especially here where I feel in danger, trapped, a slave/prisoner. I know now just how Alfred [Chester] felt in Morocco. You don't feel it's possible to leave—it's a police state with the red tape, the officials, all the difficulties—the exit visa, getting to the border, the formalities. And if I have a rug with me, the complications—needing papers for it or whatever, and will they confiscate it anyway on a technicality. I'll breathe a sigh of relief when I'm in the West again, not that officialdom there is so easy to deal with.

The French couple finally paid 100 Afs. for a truck to take them to the airport. I really felt desolate seeing them leave. I didn't like them so much, but they had each other and that made them beautiful. The two Americans drove away this morning too. I saw their car creeping along the mountain road across the river. That road is unbelievable—shored up just with twigs and stones. Now I'm all alone here and can't wait to leave tomorrow, but am terrified that I won't be able to get out. I dread the difficulties of getting to the airport and buying the ticket. Could there really be no travel agent in town, as I am told?

I made a bad mistake this morning. I told the *batcha* at the Ka-loob that it was dirty there and here it is clean—I needn't have made an enemy. Now my paranoia says he might make me trouble. I met the two *batchas* walking back from the direction of the police station and my *batcha* said I must move to the Ka-loob. Perhaps they got me in trouble. Now my batcha is nowhere to be seen. That's all I needed! I really must get out of this place.

At a shop where I was bargaining for buzkhazi stockings—I offered 100

Afs. for two pair and they wanted 120 Afs.—the men said the bookshop across the way was run by a communist. They asked if America was socialist and I said no. I asked them if the communist was a good man and they said he wasn't. I said we had communists too, but felt it politic to add that it didn't matter because we were stronger. They said I should pay more for the stockings because I'm a rich American and for me the price is low. A number of shopkeepers feel that way here, and I agree myself.

The young Afghan who has a room at the Ka-loob has a joke that makes me sick. If I ask someone's name he says it's "dung." I'm in such a depression, I wish I'd left today. There isn't a single tea house in the village that I can bear. They're all filthy and not one is located in a pleasant spot. I might as well stay in my room—it's a comfortable prison. I seem to have come this far, as far as I could go, and fallen apart. Perhaps that's good, but it's a painful experience. How I'd like someone to stroke me all over endlessly with the fingertips. My bites would feel better at least.

I went out for a few hours. The Traffic Controller invited me to visit his office—I could tell it was a semi-official summons, so I went up there. His window has a direct view of the bridge leading into town. He's a nice-seeming policeman but the visit turned quite ominous, after much innocuous conversation, when he asked for my passport. I showed him the stamp giving me permission to stay in, but he kept asking me for my visa. I finally realized what he wanted and gave him the form with my photo on it which I got at the Afghan border, which satisfied him. I also showed him my magic letter.

What his interest in me was about stemmed from a note he had from the Commandant about one of the tourists who he thought was me. Policemen are so scary. Their friendliness is half put on to draw you out. I cause suspicion because I don't look "American" and speak Farsi, which Americans never do. And I'm wandering around on my own. They keep thinking I'm some kind of spy. I had the same problem in Greece in 1949 during their revolution, where I was called into the police station wherever I went and interrogated—this actually helped me learn Greek.

Another thing I learned was that there are no planes tomorrow, so I'm leaving on the bus.

I bought a sack for my extra things, although immediately afterwards I saw nicer sacks, and later in the bazaar I was offered gorgeous saddlebags which I regretfully refused. The bag I got is a traditional rice sack in a standard size. They're hand-woven in wool with pink stripes. The natural-colored ones, in a larger size, are wheat sacks, with handsome stripes of different shades of brown and tan wool. I also bought two pairs of buzhkazi stockings, one of which cost 30 Afs. and the other 50.

I passed the shop of a silversmith who told me that my painter friend from the bus to Kundoz had been there, so I sat down and waited while his son went and fetched him. When he arrived I was glad to see a friend and showed him my room at the guest house. He's from a little village near Jurm—near, he explained, means a day's walk away. He said that the silversmith was a famous artist in his craft. I suppose I should have tried to buy something but jewelry is hard for me to pay attention to, having been brought up in a Spartan tradition.

He said the roads are so terrible here because the government doesn't allocate funds to this province like it does elsewhere, so this is a very poor area. But he says the people are considered the smartest in the whole country and when they go to Kabul they become famous. He asked me to look at his paintings when I get back to Kabul. They're mostly scenes of the country.

I'm so happy to be leaving tomorrow, and traveling by bus is really more me than the plane, which intimidates me. It seemed complicated getting out to the airfield, and I had the feeling there might not have been a seat for me when I got there. So I'll sit all day on the bus again—that is my fate. I hope we get to Kundoz tomorrow night, but if not, I'll sleep somewhere.

AUGUST 3. I'm packed and ready, but it's still too early. The bus doesn't leave until eight or nine, probably to give people time to come in from surrounding towns.

Last night I had the light on for awhile and a cloud of gnats filled the air—so it's not fleas! I sprayed and sprayed and used up my Japanese bomb. I think it has contributed to my "cold," or perhaps my "cold" is from this poison.

I woke happy to be leaving, for beautiful as it is here the vibes are bad. I'm too paranoid for this police and border scene. Could I live here for a summer? It's one of those places you'd need lots of visitors from the outside world—a small foreign colony of writers. One would be too much of a pioneer here. Like Irene Fornes at Marbella in the fifties, when she decided to spend the winter there and it was so lonely she left after three days.

The *batcha* has come in offering me tea but I've refused because his tea is vile and his kettle is black. I'd love tea and *nan*, but how can I go to a tea shop without hurting his feelings? Yesterday when I was with the French couple saying goodbye, he came running, anxious that I was also leaving (I nearly wrote "escaping"). I reassured him that I was only seeing them off. I'm quite touched by the way he's sitting in lotus-posture and looking at me, partly with affection and partly worry about the money.

He's insisting on bringing me tea. Oh, dear…I wish he was a real servant, I could tell him what to do. If I come here again, the first thing I must do is hire a servant. It would be very cheap and it would be convenient to have someone to take care of me. Why haven't I done it? I'm really a masochist.

A camel train is passing the bridge now. With a clear view of the bridge, the traffic officer can watch whatever comes into town. One of the camel trains the other day had a lead camel with his head gorgeously decorated with dangling pompoms and he knew he was special for he carried his head proudly. Each camel has a pile of mats, blankets, things, and a wife on top. That fancy camel must have carried the favorite wife.

My bruises are barely healed from the bumpy trip here. I dread the day ahead but will exult once I'm on the road, and out of here. I'm still afraid the police won't let me go. It's irrational but they're capable of complicating my departure.

Later. I'm on the road to Kundoz and we've stopped at the same serail I slept in on the way here, though this time for lunch. It's going to be a long hard trip, with these wooden seats and no springs in the bus. But I'm relieved to be on my way. I thought for a while I wouldn't be able to, because after a touching farewell with the *batcha* I was waiting for the bus when the traffic controller passed and asked me to come to his office. I couldn't tell whether it was an official summons or a personal invitation. I wanted to wait for the bus in the bazaar and talk to people. I said I was worried I might miss it, but he said the bus had to stop at the bridge for his okay before it could leave, so I had to go with him, and sat uncomfortably in his office for an hour until we saw the bus pull on to the bridge and stop.

The traffic officer spoke a little German and it turned out he attended the Police Academy in Kabul which is run or was set up by the Germans. Perhaps that's why the police are so scary here. They study German methods.

He said that if I spoke Farsi well I could pass for Afghan. My hair is like theirs, my color, my face. He said I was as close to being one of them as possible, without being it. I wondered if he would hit on the truth, for his policeman's mind was working. He didn't keep me there in his office for nothing. I was so nervous I scratched my bites and now must take myself in hand again.

The consolation was a charming young officer who, it turned out, was also going to Kundoz and he and I squeezed into the packed bus together. He's 29 and unmarried which is unusual here. Yet, although he's affectionate, I'm wondering if he hasn't been assigned to me as escort, and feel slightly nervous that he might be taking me into the police station at Kundoz. We're in a row of four seats that were already filled, making us six people in the row. But a board has been put across the aisle big enough for a child which loosens it up a little. Nobody complains of the overcrowding. My knees are raw from bumping against the metal seat ahead of me and my shoulder from rubbing against the window rails. Luckily my turban protects my head from a hard bump against the low ceiling—I wonder if the turban wasn't originally worked out to carry things on the head with. The bus is supposed to get to Khonabad at midnight, and my ass is already sore from bumping over the rocks. And I have the awful feeling that my baggage on top of the bus is being stolen, rifled, lost. I swore I wouldn't make this trip by road again. It's madness to send a bus over these roads. A jeep would be possible, but a loaded bus!

We passed an old piece of machinery rusting by the road and the word ERIE was painted on it, and I thought in Farsi, *watan-e-ma*, my country, and tears came into my eyes. I must admit that I long for my own country, though I can't think why. Ever since Faizabad I'm patriotic.

I just had marvelous bread the soldiers brought with them and shared with me. I love the custom that bread is always wrapped in a cloth. It's even carried to a meal in the cloth and taken away in the cloth. Another custom (or really superstition) is that you eat the bread right side up. People get upset if you turn it over.

I'm sticking to a bread and tea diet on the road, but I'd better eat other things soon. Kebabs are pretty safe. How I'd love yoghurt, but here it looks vile. My officer and his soldiers (who are riding on top of the bus) ate bread and tea and then a mixture of nuts, raisins, and dried mulberries. The soldiers brought it with them. Perhaps my companion is his superior's orderly. I'll be relieved to be free of him, for I keep thinking he's taking me to jail.

We stopped at Keshem again, and again I felt its good vibrations from the people, the atmosphere. They had beautiful, coarse-wool mats, the size of a small room, for about $5.00. I was also tempted to buy handsome, low boots, but the shape doesn't correspond to my feet and it would probably be horrible wearing them. I even met some of the people I made instant friends with before. The town is apparently a police checkpoint.

At stops like this, the other men always yell at me to get on the bus, that we're leaving. But I've learned to ignore them, for it's always some time before we actually go.

After feeling all day that I was under arrest, I've now decided that my policeman is really going to Kundoz on other business—I think about the jeep that fell off the mountain. Now he's crooning songs to me and I don't care—I've lost interest in him. All I want is a melon, kebabs, a shower, and a bed.

We just passed a valley where hundreds of Kuchees were camped—such handsome, dark-brown wool tents. And now we've been going mile after bumpy mile through a stony valley with a salt stream running through it. It's endlessly desolate, but I'd even like a mouthful of that salty water. Evening is falling and I can't imagine how the driver will see his way, but he performs miracles. All the drivers have to be geniuses.

We've broken down—gear box trouble—and again I've settled down on the mats in front of a serail/tea house with my sack for pillow and my jacket to cover my feet. We're about two hours from Khonabad they say, and I hope it's possible to go on in the morning. But the clutch is in pieces and there's really little chance of that.

I went into the bus to get my jacket and caused consternation for it seems that it's the quarters for women and children who were riding up front. I was reprimanded by some men standing guard and by the children, and was told severely not to return.

There's one divan here at the tea house which was appropriated by my policeman and a higher officer who also seems to be going to the hearing about the jeep, and they've spread out elaborate bedding and are asleep together.

I've been talking German with a young man who teaches at the Technion in Kabul and earns only 2000 Afs. a month. He pays 500 Afs. rent so his life is quite impoverished. Now after two years teaching he's getting a 200 Afs. raise and his next raise doesn't come for another two years. He wants to go to Germany to work and study, and become an engineer and not come back. Talking German has messed up my Farsi, for some words I know in Farsi and some in German, and end up mixing them together. He's furious with the policeman and his commandant for appropriating the divan where we were all sitting having tea, because he'd decided to sleep there, when the two of them brought over their bedding and just spread it out without a word of apology, dispossessing us. We moved, but there was only the ground to sleep on. He says they think of themselves as the men and everyone else as nothing. He's right. The police have such power that they lose their humanity. My policeman, friendly as he seemed, when I said I was going to stay at the Hotel Spinzar in Kundoz, had the nerve to ask if I had permission to stay there, meaning police permission. I was furious and said yes, yes. They would love to put police control on everything. He even asked for my knife and I said no, as usual. I notice that his body was ruined from the military posture. And the police/military mind being concerned with intimidation constantly, as these men are, ruins the soul also.

There's really nothing I need tonight except a sheet to keep off all the bugs the lamp attracts. I had bread, tea, and melon for dinner, which was fine. The others again couldn't understand my only ordering tea and bread. They kept insisting I eat lamb stew or palau or the greasy soup. Their persistence was quite annoying. They also kept saying, No sugar with tea? I said, No sugar. But oddly, they just have tea and *nan* like me. Perhaps it's that I'm an American and have the money and they don't.

I've been feeling tormented on this bus ride. It's a result of falling apart in Faisabad. I don't feel people treat me like I'm human. A "Mistah" is a curiosity, for their amusement. Another thing that's annoying is how so many people squeeze my bag, curious as to what I'm carrying with me. It's not just concern that keeps them insisting that I take sugar. What does "Mistah" mean to them?

In the morning shitting might be a problem. I have a little toilet paper in my sack, but I've never shit wearing these baggy clothes—unless I took off the pants first. Today, I pissed squatting down in a field, as they do. Luckily, I'd practiced at the hotel. So tomorrow morning will be another test.

AUGUST 4. It is dawn. Cocks are crowing. No use trying to sleep any more. We're in a desert valley. People are sleeping here and there on the ground or on rugs or mats. The women's quarters in the bus is alive with little boys. How difficult they are! They imitate me and laugh at me and call out "Mistah" constantly. Some are cute, but most lack any charm at all.

Odd that I had the fantasy most of the day that I was under arrest. Paranoia puts one in the middle of the apparat. It's gone this morning.

In the night I woke and an endless camel train was passing. It was cold and I scrunched up under my cotton jacket. I haven't had much sleep. I must remember next time to borrow, or bring along, a blanket. A smell of fresh horseshit kept coming over, but from where? Well, there's shit everywhere, of every kind. All along any stream or body of water there's human shit—people shit where they can wash off afterwards. And the animals graze everywhere leaving piles of it. It all dries up and blows with the dust in the wind.

I've figured out the hierarchy on the bus. The Commandant is the portly man in western clothes who sat up by the chauffeur carrying a briefcase on his lap importantly. My policeman, the aide of the Commandant on this mission, sits in the middle of the bus in his uniform. The soldiers of his escort sit on the roof and in the back of the bus in their usual shabby *poilu* outfits, flies unbuttoned. I noticed the soldiers went off into the darkness and spent the night out in the fields together.

God knows when the engine will be put together so we can leave. I have a hunch that although they claim to have found a broken part, they could have continued with the journey, but didn't want to go further on this bad road in the darkness. The gear box is sitting like a wreck on a mat in the dust, pieces of the shattered gear next to it. They're waiting for a spare part to come from Taluquan. But this might be standard—they might always find one excuse or another to stay overnight here and the bus driver gets a payoff from the teashop keeper.

I feel filthy. Most of the men have washed, but I can't do it at the river. I shit, using my toilet paper. But it was beyond my squatting talents to balance at the edge of the stream and reach down to scoop up water.

One mustn't ever show the drawstring in Afghani pants. Mine was hanging below my shirt tail and it was called to my attention. Sitting down, one must be careful to pull the front shirt flap over the crotch. Another drawstring problem is that when I untie it to lower my pants to pee, an end of the tie gets lost in the large waistband, and I haven't learned the technique of pulling it through without a clip or pin. I'm sure there's a simple way it's done, perhaps keeping it from slipping away by tying it to a stick.

A Kuchee camel train just passed and I got a look at the women riding on the camels. They're ravishingly beautiful. They wear quite heavy silver jewelry all over their heads, shoulders and arms, and black, gold-embroidered shawls—most of them make only a bare attempt to hide their faces. The children ride on one camel, wives on others. The old women look back boldly as I stare. The patriarch rides by on a horse holding a boy. His eyes are blue. The Kuchee men are all grey-bearded, it seems. The camels' tails are tied by braided rope to the next camel's halter. I can't tell the gender of the camels—none of them seems to have anything between their legs. The horses have pulsating assholes as they move.

There seem to be endless caravans passing, each with three or four camels. The Kuchees must move every day—I think they go all the way to the Pamir mountains in summer. They're camped over just down the road. I'd like to visit them. Dare I walk over? It's the dogs I'm afraid of.

I saw them preparing the samovar in the teashop. There's a vertical fuel pipe through the center of the water cylinder of the samovar which is filled with wood and ignited, the ashes falling below and an extension for smoke leading up to the roof. Water is poured into the cylinder around the hot pipe which brings it to a boil.

The buildings in this part of the world often have quite beautiful front porches. The roof hangs over supported by three or five stripped poles. It's almost Japanese in its simplicity.

I just made an awful mistake. A car carrying French people passed, going in our direction and I was asked to speak to them and ask them to take me to Taluquan and get a spare gear there. But my bus mates were speaking excitedly and I didn't understand—I thought I was being asked to read instructions on the American engine that nobody else could read. So when the car went by, I didn't run after it with the others and nobody could make the French understand what we needed. I saw everyone running after the car, and I wasn't going to join them gawking at the foreigners. It was only after the car had left that the German-speaking boy told me what they had wanted of me. Nobody seems to hold it against me that I didn't speak to them, probably because I'm exempt from human responsibility. I feel resentful that they don't ask why I didn't help.

It looks like we're here for the day. The driver and his helper have to wait for a car to come our way, and few vehicles come through this long, stony valley. Then get a lift to Taluqan to buy the part, and then find a ride back, and finally fix the motor. That should take five or six hours minimum.

The village I really like in this part of the world is Keshem. Why couldn't we have broken down there? One thing I promise myself if we're here in the heat of the day, I'm going to get my towel out of my valise and go swimming in the river.

Everybody is eating breakfast and seems cheerful. I shouldn't be so private, but all that speaking German has ruined my concentration on Farsi.

Questions one is always asked: Where are you going? Where are you from? What is your name? If they speak a little English it can be confusing because they ask, Where do you live, and you don't know what they mean. I prefer to say, at the hotel, until they clarify. Where are you going is also cryptic for they often mean to Pakistan or India, instead of to the bazaar. Another most important question, which is often the first is, What do you want? This seems rude to me but to them seems obvious.

More camels passing, a three-camel caravan. A young woman in a red velvet shawl on the front camel, an old woman behind, and the last camel carrying tent poles. The camels have odd, soft, two-toed feet and rabbit mouths.

Well, I don't want to be in Kabul so badly. Mail? It will only make me unhappier.

They aren't taking my money here, making me feel guiltier. Last night as I lay here looking at the stars, far from home, my grief came over me. What is there to miss? Whatever that is, it's home.

If everyone wants my knife, I ought to give it away and take the local knife in exchange. And trade my watch for one of theirs. That would simplify things.

This breakdown is like a self-fulfilling prophecy. I felt I couldn't escape, the stars were against my leaving. I really am a little crazy now. A crying jag I had the other day was the biggest crying jag since the Caspian Sea. Both were significant.

I'd like to go off by myself. I wonder if it would be safe?

I went down the river a way and took a bath in the river which helped some. I came back to find a jeep leaving for Taluqan. I could have taken my baggage and gone with it. Why didn't I? Am I such a masochist? Some sense of belonging with the others? I must take the next vehicle that comes by.

I've been trying to study Farsi by reading the Arabic script from my children's reader, but people keep looking on and reading for me. I've stopped being polite and just move away to another place. They must think me very strange by now. A little boy of about eleven has been following me about, annoying me intensely. He couldn't be cuter, but he's a pest.

I notice that my right heel is cut on the bottom, perhaps from nails in my sandals. I'll have to attend to it when I get to town. I really feel crummy sitting here in this tea house with the flies and the little boy, but the one green place with trees has been appropriated by some nomads who set up their tents next to it. It's only nine-thirty and I'm already suicidal. They say a rescue truck is coming but I'm skeptical.

A boy is playing the *tambour*, a three-string instrument like a *bouzouki* with a small body and long neck. And I just realized this is teaching me something—it's very good to lie around here waiting for the relief truck. I've been fighting it, but this as good a thing to do as anything, as good a place to be as anywhere. There's a pleasant breeze, I'm in the shade, someone is singing and playing the *tambour*. I can go bathe in the river again, the people are okay if not thrilling, and there's bread and tea. Where else in the world can one lie around on the floor this way? And the wind has blown the flies into hiding. If anyone I know in America could see me here like this they'd be amazed. How I resist just taking life as it comes! It's better here than Kundoz. And why hurry back to Kabul? I was dying of frustration a little while ago—and now? Now I am content:

Yes, one place is as good as another.

Kundoz. I can't believe I'm here at last. A truck came along and everybody asked our bus driver to refund some of the fare they'd paid so that they could take the truck to Taluqan and not have to pay twice to get there. He wouldn't do it, so they all stayed behind but me, the rich American who could afford to do such an extravagant thing. Saying goodbye, my policeman kissed me twice.

The truck was horrible. The men in back with me discussed my possible wealth and I wondered if I was going to be assaulted and robbed, but it didn't happen. I resumed my vile mood—I was a nasty American to everyone. In Taluqan I asked people to leave me alone, to go away. When I ate kabobs there I asked the kabobs man to go buy me a melon. First, he brought me back a big one for seven Afs. and I said no, I wanted a small one for four Afs., so he went back, grumpily, for he was the proprietor and not used to being ordered about in the tone I have today. He overcharged me for the kabobs but I didn't object, I deserved it. Some students were watching me eat and I ordered them to go away. I suddenly couldn't stand the "Mistahs" and the questions about where I was from, etc. When they ask me where I'm from, I either don't answer or say the United States, which always confuses them. They only understand America. So now I'm explaining about Canada and Mexico being America too, but they know better because I'm simply an American to them.

The next stage of the journey was a jeep from Taluqan to Khonabad, which is supposed to take two hours but took nearer three. It was packed, and there was no room for my feet, and I had to hold my valise between my knees. They squeeze an amazing number of people in—the seat is just a bench on either side. So my ass is really sore tonight. There were a group of students aboard whom I felt were making fun of me and I was also nasty to them. When one said where was I going, I said he knew where the jeep was going so where else would I be going? And when another asked me what was in my suitcase I said dollars, I was that sassy.

I saw hashish growing along the fields usually bordering cotton or corn which had a large, white mallow-like flower, very different from the variety I grew on my windowsill.

The jeep from there to Kundoz was also packed and had equally unpleasant people. One man who was really evil, flicked my valise with his finger asking what was in it. I made believe I didn't know a word of Farsi on that ride. This irritability is perhaps from poor diet. They always say lack of B vitamins leads to irritability and the diet has been slim. I ate kabobs for lunch, but tonight I'm just eating tomatoes and grapes and drinking limeade.

The roads were bad the whole way. The trip took till about six-thirty, so I don't see how the broken-down bus will make it before ten or eleven, if at all today. As I left on the truck, the people had just returned with the new gear. Assembling the gear box and the installation surely would take two hours at least.

My rice sack was open when I got it off the bus roof so it was obviously looked into. I haven't yet checked to see if everything is here.

I took two carriage rides today, one in Khonabad because it really is a long way from the jeep station where we arrived from Taluqan across town to the jeep station to Kundoz, but I shared it and it only cost five Afs. On the way I saw marvelous shops that made me want to stay another day in Khonabad to go shopping. The bazaar looks more interesting than the one here. When I got to Kundoz, I took another horse and buggy to the hotel, which cost ten Afs.

Here, I feel like I've escaped from the police blockade. It was so good to get away from Faizabad and finally from my policeman. Although I did go for him in a way. At the end he kept redoing my turban, because he said I didn't put it on well. I think Faizabad men have bigger pricks than anywhere else in Afghanistan. They seemed to be swinging low all over the place, whereas everywhere else it's hardly a bulge. Maybe their baggy pants are made differently.

I dreamed of getting the room with the fan that the American boy had, and was happy when I found it empty, but the fan was no longer working, and though I was assured another fan would be brought in I was dubious about that. But tonight I spoke to the *batcha* again and lo, he came in with a working fan.

In the bazaar a lot of people welcomed me back and it made me feel good. One man gave me a melon for my room. Lots of people wanted to know where was my *lunghi*, and I explained how dirty my Afghani clothes were. They all said to wash them tonight.

I asked about a taxi to Kabul tomorrow, but though the agents promised me that they had five people and only needed a sixth to make a load, and the sixth would be me, I was skeptical. I've heard them calling out for hours for passengers to fill the taxi to Kabul. I went to the bus office and found only three places were left, on the rear hard seat. This wasn't possible, considering the state of my behind after this two-day trip. So when three of the awful students from the jeep came into the bus office, I let them have the three seats.

Then I went back and found another taxi driver who also said he had five persons and only needed me to fill up the cab, a Volga, and was leaving at five-thirty a.m. and would pick me up at the hotel. I told him okay, if it was true. I'm sure it wasn't, and when he picks me up at that time he'll say the others will be coming or have canceled, and it will be hours before we leave. If this happens, I hope I have the nerve to desert him for a fuller taxi. It's all very chancy. I know I've been sold a bill of goods. It's in his interest to tell me this story. Anyway, waking at that time is not too hard anymore and I can always sit with friends at my breakfast tea house. The driver makes it all sound rosy, that we'll be in Kabul at one o'clock. That really would be nice. I could even get to the American Embassy by four for my mail. The taxi costs two hundred Afs., which seems extravagant. It feels like I've been spending lots of money.

I still don't know when the Muslims get circumcised, or if all of them do here. Some little boys seem to have foreskins, but when men were questioning me one day about whether I was a Muslim, one of them asked a question I didn't understand and made the sign of a knife cutting across the penis which made it clear.

Another thing I'm still uncertain about—what do they have in mind when I say I'm a *shah-er*, a poet? I've been asked to sing one of my songs sometimes, so they connect it with music. Here it must be an almost mythical tradition, although some people have been introduced to me as *shah-ers*. One old man was a dervish *shah-er*; I'd like to have gone to his house. When I was asked how long it took me to become a *shah-er*, I said until I was thirty-eight when my book was published. But the word is said with such awe I feel like a complete phony.

The engineer who lives in the hotel across the hall was glad to see me again, and when I told him how the people of Badakshan resent the fact that the government doesn't spend any money there, he said that there was no good economic reason to invest money there. Here there is industry and the government makes money. I suppose from taxes. But there they pay few taxes.

He told me that he graduated from the engineering faculty in Kabul a few years ago and served two years in the army afterward. But he couldn't study all that time and feels he has gotten behind if he wants to go abroad to get his Master's degree. He asked me if I could recommend a good engineering school in the U.S. with low tuition. The schools he has applied for say that after one term he can get an assistantship, but the problem is the money to get there and live the first half year. I gave him my idea about getting scholarships if you really go after one.

When my fan didn't work he said that will mean his workshop would get it to fix tomorrow—he seems to be in charge of things like that. He's now working toward the Independence Day festival when they're going to have a huge camp ground, and he wants to make a big sign with words spelled out in electric lights listing the products of the town, each flashing on, one after the other. He speaks good English—he really understands it—and I'm sure he'll have no problem getting a scholarship in the U.S. He was offered one in the Soviet Union during his undergraduate years but turned it down. He told me this when I suggested that these scholarships for students from underdeveloped countries were a way of winning over minds to our way of life. He quickly said that he was already won over. Yet the young teacher on the bus from Faizabad with whom I spoke in German said all the students wanted socialism.

I must say that back in Kundoz I feel at home. I know people already and I could probably stay on. But I'd better go back to Kabul and eat eggs every day and carrot juice and try to gain some weight.

AUGUST 5. Dawn. I always seem to be getting up at dawn here. I'm even sorer this morning, but how I slept! Like the dead. My foot feels bad. I should have washed it with soap again. But in Kabul tonight, if I ever get there, I'll get some iodine. I also had a bottle of the local lemon soda which was syrupy sweet. I've taken three charcoal pills to get me through the journey, but there is a lot of gurgling going on and I wonder.

I'm spending so much today—hotel, taxi, then there'll be a cab to my hotel in Kabul. I really regret not staying here another day. I'm so sore, even the taxi to Kabul will be a little difficult—if it comes. He's already late. I suspect it will be a good long time before he shows.

"Volga" here is almost synonymous with taxi, and *samovar* is an alternate word for teahouse. But when I said that *darya*—river—as in Amu Darya must be Russian too, people denied it.

Maybe I was foolish to try to go to Kabul today, I'm so tired. Will the Volga never come?

It came—a miracle—and after a few delays for gas (gas costs 6 Afs. a liter here, that's only seven cents!), picking up cans of films from the movie house, a stop for melons, we are off. But the melons were too expensive, ten Afs. for the big ones, so we're on the lookout now.

The Volga has a Japanese refrigerator filling the back seat and with just three of us in front I can't believe I'm going to Kabul in such luxury. The way it works is that the refrigerator and its owner sitting next to me are taking up five places in the car, that's 1,000 Afs. The cab as a whole would cost 1200 Afs., the standard price. So with my 200 Afs. the driver isn't losing anything. And he'll make a little on the film and melons—there are quite a few of them in the cab already. The car is heavily loaded though, and there will be frequent stops for water.

The driver spits into a little silver chalice which I've seen before, perhaps in Indian movies.

We're now coming to the first hills and there's a village of cave dwellers. Perhaps now the caves are used mostly for livestock and storage, because there are lots of mud-brick, fortress-type houses below.

We passed an encampment of tents below the road where some trucks were parked and the driver said it was a place where you can fuck women. The Farsi word he used was *kuss* like in German. I asked about whores in Kabul and he said there were none, but there were in Herat. He said to have one costs from 20 to 40 Afs. The word that he gave me for whore was *mordaligau*, which sounds like "dead cow."

The man who's bringing the refrigerator to Kabul is only twenty and not yet married, but he seems to be one of those high-charged businessmen—he always has to be turning on the radio or something. He says he'll go to Moscow on business, buying and selling. The flight from Moscow to here costs 20,000 Afs., but only 10,000 Afs. from here to there.

They just told me they heard Nixon was dead on the radio, but it turns out it was a joke (*mazak*). I don't think it was funny. I really got scared what it would mean politically. These things must seem far away from their lives.

A boy was selling a huge gutted fish by the road and the driver stopped, but the boy wanted 50 Afs. and the driver offered 10 Afs.—which was refused, so he drove on.

We're at a teahouse restaurant on the Salang road. The water is sparkling clean, so I drank a little and washed my face and even waded in it, but my feet got too cold. This would not be a bad place to stay a few days except that everyone comes and goes and it would be hard to stay put. There is even a dervish here with his patched coat. When I ask my companions if it's true that this road over the Hindu Kush and the Salang tunnel were built by the Russians, they say yes, but the road from Kabul to Kandahar was built by the Americans, and the Kabul/Djellalabad road was built by the Germans.

The driver got onto politics which made me nervous. He said that Russia was arming "Arabstan" and America was arming Israel and that it was not good that they should fight. I was relieved he took that position for it is mine and I agreed.

I find myself still hung up on "getting there," and I'm itching to get on to Kabul. I wish I could learn to go with things, for "here" is a special experience too. There are mulberries that I wish I dared eat. I would if I hadn't been so loose this morning. I can see that the drivers like to stay up here at Salang as long as possible. They linger, all of them, as long as they can. We're going to stop again much higher up and eat my melon. Perhaps our driver will even get a piece of ice to bring down to Kabul. I'm really very lucky to have gotten this cab, for the other cabs from Kundoz at the stop were chock full of people, children, merchandise, etc.

We've made another stop higher up and are having my melon. Everyone wants to trade watches with me and knives. But I remain adamant. Though the chauffeur's Russian watch is tempting with its twenty-one jewels.

Why does Salang make everyone sleepy? The altitude? I always get drowsy and now the driver is nodding off. We have to keep him awake. Luckily we've now stopped for the chauffeur to sleep.

The Russians have put up mileage posts, really kilometer posts, showing the distance to and from the Russian border. We are now passing the 354 kilometer point, a half hour from Kabul. The driver told me the place to get laid in Kabul is at Darowdi Lowri—20 Afs. a throw. I must go there and see.

I think the reason I slip into German so easily and find it hard to get back to Farsi is that they are both so gutteral. Farsi is actually more guttural. I think my cab mates are speaking with a kind of lisp as well. The driver perhaps because he has *aswar* under his tongue, or perhaps they speak Pashtoo frequently, or have a local accent. The tongue seems thick and up front.

Kabul. How slowly the cab went toward the end, but finally we got in to Kabul. My young businessman, it turns out, was scared shitless, never having been to Kabul before. I parted warmly from him and the driver, kissing them both. I was surprised the driver kissed me on the mouth. I had the feeling toward the end that he was trying to think of some way to cheat me and I was prepared to fight for my rights. But if it was in his mind, he did nothing. It could have been my paranoia, but I looked in his palm and saw the heart line bent toward the head line.

I took a cab to the Tourist Hotel. I find my Farsi is much better now than before and I can tell the drivers how to go. But everyone is amazed I know so much after only six weeks. The little book is really quite good.

At the hotel the proprietor and I kissed warmly and he gave me a Coca Cola. I made the mistake of not kissing the manager Joseph, who has been distant ever since. Then the patron of the hotel sent a fancy cake of soap to my room, and the towel and the sheets were clean. Also a bottle of water without my having to ask.

I'm now eating at my garden kabob restaurant. The people are so good here. They put their hands to their hearts sincerely when greetings are said. I too do that. I saw four soldiers kissing on the street. One glanced at me, a trifle self-consciously I thought. The most intense flirtations are around the Park Cinema where most of the boys are in slacks and shirts. Odd, I'm getting called after very little lately.

The thing about Kabul is it just looks ramshackle. Today it is blowy and the hills look very near.

I took a cab to and from the embassy to get my mail. It was a necessary extravagance and I felt secure enough to tell the cab driver the fare was only 20 Afs. when he asked for more.

My big disappointment tonight was that neither the hotel nor the restaurant had carrot juice, but I was happy to learn that the restaurant has yoghurt. Unfortunately, I can't stand the yoghurt. I wish I could eat the food here, but the taste is entirely alien to me and unhealthy. The kabobs have made me a little sick. I don't think I can ever eat kabobs again. I looked in the mirror and saw a hollow-cheeked wraith, like an escapee from prison. I must find something I can eat. Chicken at the Khyber? I must indulge myself as much as possible. I think I'll buy some tomatoes and eat them in my room.

I'm so tired I'm dropping, but maybe I'll go to see the French movie here at the Park Cinema, *Man of Marrakesh*, which I've always wanted to see. Or tomorrow.

I wonder if my nastiness recently is the true me coming out. I'm nice because I go in fear. When I'm not so scared I don't have to be nice. The driver today was a man of very good temper and perfect digestion. Most of the chauffeurs on buses and jeeps and Volgas are very sweet people. The driver of the truck to Faisabad was nice too. When I was at the hotel he wanted me to come sleep with them at the *serail*, perhaps to sleep with him.

Is the male genital thing at some kind of high level of intensity in Turkey and then tapers off to the East? Here, you don't feel the genitals thrust at you, nor in Iran. And surely in India and eastwards, there isn't the genital emphasis. It is relaxing to be away from the genital competition of the West.

I had some trouble getting a 500 Afs. note changed, but then bought tomatoes and grapes. They're effectively killing the strong mutton taste of the kabobs. I nearly bought the Weekly Guardian to read before bed, but resisted. I've avoided the news successfully so far this summer. But today's false alarm about the death of Nixon made me anxious. What have I to do with all that? I don't know, but I care, as I found out the other day. It took me till forty-six to get the feeling it was my country.

AUGUST 6. I'm eating pale fried eggs at the Khyber. It feels so good to wake up and have firm bowels and to speak enough Farsi to feel at home. And on the bus, knowing the fare, where to get off. I threw the waiter just now by trying to order in Farsi. He looked as though I were crazy and got flustered. In this place it just won't do. And the morning is cool, the fountain playing. The wind yesterday brought cool weather.

It really is only a week away that I want to leave—it's hard to realize. My visa will have to be extended a week. And the problem of mailing things will have to be attacked immediately. All these things I bought and need to send. Maybe I'll try mailing something today. I'll go now and buy wrapping paper and string.

I think I must give up on these sandals and try another pair. The nails keep coming up and my heels are cut up and sore.

I passed the shop where the boy sold me a piece of opium some time ago, and again he came out and asked if I wanted hashish. But as I asked the word for opium in Farsi—always the student—the boy suddenly started offering me tomatoes. I turned and saw an officer had stopped in for something, so I said I didn't want any and left. I must go back and see if he has any clean opium.

First success—at the central post office I had to open the parcel with the stockings that I had tried to mail in Kundoz, but otherwise mailing them was easy. Forty grams cost 44 Afs.

In the post office I met an interesting African-American man named Lafayette Bozeman. He was mailing a manuscript to Grove Press, so I added a note to my old editor Richard Seaver to his letter. We went for tea and he told me he was living in a house in Paghman with an upper-class English girl. The rent is 1500 Afs. a month. He's been all over Asia, and once was repatriated forcibly. Anyway, he says he didn't have to pay the fare. He talks very high-falutin metaphysics, but beyond the bullshit he's into good things. And he's an Aquarian, so my instinctive taking to him was right. But he's used to using people to keep going since he has no income or really any way of earning money as far as I can see. Somehow he manages. I noticed he came on to all the white chicks—no, that's unfair, because all there are here are white girls. Anyway, he tunes right in to their sexuality and doesn't mind being brushed off. He seems to be breaking up with his girlfriend so perhaps that's why he was so aggressive. I asked him what he did and he said he wasn't really a writer. The book he was sending to Grove Press was on metaphysics—in the West he'd be called a metaphysician and in the east a yogi. He invited me to visit him in Paghman, but the instructions to get to his house are complicated and I wonder if I'd find him.

I walked him back to the Khyber. In little ways Bozeman used me. First, he asked me to buy him an airmail envelope for his cover letter and I went out and got one. He didn't even offer to pay for it. But I treated him to tea anyway. I'm sure he has a hard time financially. He talks about "good family," so that's another of his hang-ups.

I found wrapping paper, string, plastic bags and muslin bags, came home and wrapped and addressed all the things I'd bought. Then I took one of the packages to the post office—it was the stockings and shawl which I put in a plastic bag inside a muslin bag. After the postal official inspected it I sewed it up. I now have five paper parcels to send. The official is my friend now and I hope he won't make me unwrap them all. I only loosely tied them, just in case. Tomorrow is the sabbath and the post office is closed so I'll go on Saturday.

I also assembled a bagful of my own things to mail home, so I don't have to lug everything around with me. September is quite chilly in Europe but I don't think I'll suffer too much on my way back. If Yugoslavia is cold, I'll buy something warm there. Dubrovnik anyway will be warm. And I'll have to carry a blanket for the boat. Maybe a camel's hair or one of those cheap quilts. Perhaps I'd better have a sleeping sack made up before I leave.

I've washed my clothes, in case I go to Paghman tomorrow. I really need a cloth to lie down on. Everyone uses them for a shawl, a sheet, a bread wrapper, a towel—they're quite useful.

I went from the post office to the market near the mosque and bought tomatoes, cucumbers, red grapes and that dark loaf bread I discovered here—I think it must be like Russian bread. Back at the hotel I asked the boy about the cork I had holding the window open which is gone—my last one. The other also was taken by the boy. But he played dumb and even laughed at my annoyance.

I'm at the restaurant at the Helal Hotel that several people have recommended. The room is full of the world-traveling young, of whom I'm not one. The menu looks promising. There's even apple pie. I ordered chicken which is apt to be less greasy. The service is more western than usual, with the waiter laying out my silver and napkins like any restaurant. The soup unfortunately has that muttony taste I'm allergic to. But there are real vegetables in it and it feels good in my stomach. How I long for cooked beets, zucchini, corn, which don't exist here.

I feel like Craig Claiborne reporting on this restaurant: The food is quite good. The baked potato had delicious herb butter on it and though the chicken is over-fried I'm eating it like an animal and enjoying it. One should eat like an animal. Why, though, is chicken the most expensive thing on the menu here? In Europe too. I notice everybody is ordering steak, which is cheaper.

When I left the hotel I spoke briefly to Joseph the manager and he complained to me about his salary which is only 2000 Afs. a month and no future. On that he supports his family who live in a house in Shari Nau—he said the rent was 600 Afs. a month. But he could open a little hotel for 50,000 Afs. He would rent a house with a kitchen and furnish it, then rent out rooms and allow the guests to do their own cooking and take care of themselves, and charge very little rent. He's so smart, I am sure he'll do it. I'd like to give him the money. Maybe if I make lots this year. His father is sick and he supports the whole family, but he feels so poor and frustrated. He'd like to get out of the country for awhile. There was a chance he could go to Australia or Holland but it fell through. I asked him to get me the words for the song "Chamoli" but he never heard of it. How Afghan is he? There is such a turning away from traditional things on the part of the modern young.

There are two fans turning lazily overhead but the breeze doesn't get to my table. The Afghans in the room look like gangsters. I must say I enjoyed the meal. Tomorrow I ought to check the Kabul Hotel dining room, or maybe go to Bagh e Bala. Or if I'm at Paghman maybe there's a good restaurant there.

The fountain was gorgeous tonight, a sharp wind blowing it to spray and the moon with its dog star through the mist. The mosque of the bazaar had a red light on top of the minaret, a beautiful note against the sky. Everything looked pretty. The modern buildings fronting the park appeared neat for once and the park with its onion-dome pavilion seemed clean and rural. It's a trick of the light, that some days the city looks beautiful. Since coming back everyone looks so sexy too. I wish I were staying and opening a hotel with Joseph.

I must come back here for breakfast. The men all look like desperadoes— outlaws from western movies. The French tend to look the most authentic. I could cast a western movie easily from this room. The women would look great too. The room is really quite pleasant, though the plastic tablecloths ruin the effect. And the dirty cement floor. Very few flies, but that's because the windows are closed and you pay for it by being hot. Why not end this review by Craig Claiborne with the lemon pie I'm having for dessert?

The pie was a complete flop. Not lemony at all. It should have been called lemon-colored pie. What this town lacks is an elegant pastry shop like Porte's in Tangier.

Thank God there's no tipping in this country. But the poor waiters look so underpaid. Well, everyone is, here. Yet how can people afford those silk lunghis for 400 Afs. or those silk coats for 8000 Afs.?

I asked the doorman where the Darwazil Lowri and the Daraudi Lowri were, but he said they were far, although he seemed not to know where they were. A well-dressed man then chimed in and asked why I wanted to go there. I said there was the Faroukhi Theater in Darwazil Lowry. He said there was no theater there, only in Chaman and the Marastown Theater in Daria. I said I'd been told there was, and he said it was dangerous for a foreigner to go into Darwazil Lowri at night. I'll have to go first during the day. I didn't have the nerve to tell him that I was curious about the prostitutes in Daraudi Lowri.

A young man joined me on my way home, obviously trying to pick me up. He's living at the Pamir Hotel where his bed costs 30 Afs. a night. When I avoided his clutching hand he told me a ridiculous story of meeting a woman in the park at Shari-nau for a night of drinking and dancing and screwing. Why didn't I like him? Because he was in western clothes that made him look dumpy? He was twenty-three and a student, he said. I ought to be flattered, but I feel a cold coming on and don't feel at all romantic. I brushed him off and came home. I think I ought to just stay in bed tomorrow.

This is a country for the adventurous young. It's perfect for them. They set up an international beatnik/hippie atmosphere that they are happy in, and that fits into the ways of the country well. The rich tourists are completely out of place and only disturb the economy.

AUGUST 7. How time is passing. I'll be leaving in about a week. I've awakened at dawn with a sore throat. I think I've got to be out of the country before Jeshin, the Independence Day Festival on the 18th, which lasts several days. If I get the packages mailed, that will be a big step. And I ought to allow a week for the whole trip—at least 24 hours to go to Herat and another day across the border. Perhaps I should stop in Kandahar on the way. I keep thinking I'll buy stuff in Herat and Kandahar.

I have a feeling I'm going to fly across Iran from Erzurum to Tabriz and avoid Tehran completely, and miss the long desert rides. I must find out where to get the boat for Cyprus. Perhaps tomorrow I should go to the Turkish embassy. No wonder I woke up at dawn.

I learned that the wrapping paper I've been using is Japanese. It's amazing that there are products from all over the world in this little country. But where does it get the foreign exchange to pay for all this stuff? Maybe that's why it is so poor. The one thing you don't see are a lot of international newspapers and magazines shops, for nobody reads.

I'm having breakfast at the hotel and afterwards I'm going right back to bed. I'm even more tired than I thought from my trip. I feel I might fall down if I don't lie down. How to be really good to myself? Buy a can of Kandahar grape juice? Or a kilo of the most beautiful grapes I can find. Cookies too. I wonder if there's a new Guardian Weekly out today.

Breakfast is taking so long in coming I feel like going somewhere else. But there, I'm still going too fast. What's the difference how long it takes? Remember the lesson in the desert.

Breakfast came and is so bad I'd like to send it back. Eggs cold and yokes broken. Cold white bread—the toaster is on the blink, the *bacha* said. I am never going to eat here again. I just checked my money. I've got $1300 which means I've spent $400 this summer so far. How could I have so much left? Well, it will go faster once I leave this country.

I realize I'm not well, but I'm having another chicken dinner at the Helal. The Faiz had too many flies.

I think this place attracts gangsters, for a sensational-looking, tall, young man has come in, the perfect lead in a juvenile gangster movie of the 30s's. He started out a bright student with dreams of becoming a lawyer until his father was arrested on a bum rap and his life savings went to the lawyer, so the son turns into a petty hoodlum. But he's too serious for the others in the gang, being so morosely handsome.

I'm less friendly since my trip north. It was symbolic, my going as far as I could. Now I need people less maybe. Or perhaps the reason I'm not responding to anyone is that I'm ill. I'm going home after dinner and resisting the temptation of seeing "Man of Marrakesh."

An American girl from California with an indefinite accent just had a big problem over the food here because she's vegetarian and the rice is made with the invariable sheep fat. She finally settled for baked potatoes with butter. The fact that butter is from an animal doesn't bother her, so long as the animal isn't killed.

After I finished dinner—and it didn't seem as good as the night before—I joined the American girl, who was sitting with a Swedish boy with whom she sometimes traveled, she said, when I asked if they were "together." He was a young engineer who'd quit his job and gone traveling, but now after four months he had to go back and get a job. He looked like the conventional bourgeois student in his cute shirt, whereas she had gone sartorially Indian. I asked why she left most of her vegetable plate untouched, and she said if she didn't like the look of the food she didn't eat. She's been in India where it's easy to be a vegetarian. On her way there she lived on oranges, bread, and tea. I said I'd be glad for that diet if only there were oranges, as there'd been the winter when she came through. I haven't seen any lately though. And even the little withered mangos have disappeared. She really looks terrible, but that may not just be from the diet.

I found her touching with her high aesthetic manner—she studied various artistic disciplines at UCLA before going abroad. She'd been away from home four years, had spent her first year in Israel and regretted letting them stamp her passport which made it impossible for her to go to Damascus. But she said I could still go through Syria and Iraq on my passport since my name wasn't Jewish. She's spent the last six months in India, sleeping in temples, living the life of a *sadhu*. After living in India, she says she never wants to go back home. She's heading to Denmark to work, to teach, because she's running out of money, her savings from working as a librarian. She said you could get work in Bombay as a movie extra and earn 40 rupees a day, which is a lot of money in Indian terms, about $4 in our own. But she was turned down because she looks too unusual. Her Swedish friend wouldn't have any trouble—they like conventional-looking people. But I pointed out to her that in the Indian movie I saw the extras in the London nightclub scene were definitely odd birds, right out of the hippie hotel. Perhaps they were the least unusual people the director could find.

She said the men here were animals and she hated the Muslim world. I said it was better than the Christian world at least, and she said, wait till you see the Hindu world. Indian food was the purest in the world. I suggested that Japanese food was also pretty terrific. I asked if she didn't find Afghanistan quite all right for a foreign woman alone and she said yes. So I said that here the sexuality was more Eastern, where men don't always have to prove their virility, but Turkey and Iran were western where they do. I warned her that if she was going to travel through Iran and Turkey I didn't think it was safe for her. She said she came through in the winter and managed, but agreed it might be more dangerous now in summer. I gave her Clifford Wright's address in Denmark and told her of his hospitality toward artists of all nations. But sensitive about her independence, she said that she wasn't destitute, her father sent her something every month, for he worried about her.

I left feeling gassy and ill, and outside realized I hadn't paid and returned. The waiter hadn't even noticed!

A lot of people are crying to me lately. There's a little boy who sometimes approaches me as I come out the hotel, putting on the waterworks and working them up quite effectively as he tells a sad tale. He's thoroughly professional. The manager gave me his own sad story, and now the *bacha* is constantly telling me his tooth troubles and holding his head. In the country, various old men came to me with their ailments, assuming I was a doctor. One man I gave charcoal pills to, but then everyone came to me wanting pills.

AUGUST 12. My last day in Kabul. I wake alone in my room with my suitcase. The zipper looks slightly menacing. All those teeth. I've done what I always wanted to do—I came to Afghanistan.

Riding the bus into the center of town, I was peering at a magazine a fat old man was holding and it was Paris Match—an omen. He was a diploma engineer from the Sorbonne, he announced with great pride. But when I asked if he was on his way to work, he said he was retired—they don't need engineers, he had the wrong ideology. I asked if he was a Socialist, and he said no, a Republican! Which here means anti-monarchist.

Some strange-looking women were sitting by us, unveiled, with many thin braids. I asked about them because they were begging and he shouted something in Pashtoon at them. When I said weren't they poor, he said they were gypsies—and had cattle and sold the milk and butter, and they were all thieves. They got off the bus and I noticed one woman was crying, perhaps from his insults. I really liked them—they had lean, long, dark faces.

I think the bank rate for the dollar must be sensational today because the street moneychangers are offering 82 Afs. to the dollar and they're all over the place. They race by saying "Change money?" in little voices. The bank today is full of barefoot tourists. The clothes situation here is like in Miami—the tourists are dressed for holidays and the locals are trying to be formal. Though luckily the native costumes also give the scene a fantastic quality. But here in the bank the yearning for western clothes of the locals is most touching, contrasted with the Westerners' self-assurance and their freedom to wear any old thing. But even here in the bank the Afghans are walking around holding hands.

The cashier has gone on a coffee break, it seems, and we're all waiting in line.

Afghanistan, the Land of the Open Fly. But it doesn't matter—you never see anything because everyone is wearing baggy pajamas underneath.

Two young men sat down at my table for lunch, telephone operators in the PTT. They were quite disillusioned, for they felt the problem was the King. I told them my theory that they could get scholarships to study abroad—they had both finished twelfth year in high school—but they say that everyone comes back saying the US government is good, the country is good, and the people are good, and they don't want to be brainwashed like that. I told them they could keep their eyes open and not be brainwashed, but they say it's only good to go as a tourist with no government control, and to go at all from here is so difficult in any case. They had a basic hopelessness that defeated them.

My stomach is better today, and I hope it survives the hospitality ahead—both the afternoon visit to my dervish who is bound to serve fruit and sweets, and the dinner at the Tarakis. One of the boys in the Helal was squeezing lemon into his soup. He said you put it in everything when your stomach is upset. If only it would neutralize the sheep fat. But nothing will. Sheep fat rules the menu. One trouble with this country is if you get sick it's hard to get well again. Life is hard here and it's easy to go under. I hope I'm getting out in time.

The man on the bus this morning said it was a hot, dry summer because there was little snow last winter. And the girl at the mail desk at the embassy (who was at my poetry reading at Skidmore College, it turned out) said, when I told her I was coming back in the spring, that there would be a lot of mud. May, she said, was all right—things dried up by then.

I'm about to go to my master dervish. How sad I don't belong here, and how lucky I am to be able to leave.

The dervish's son, Abdul Rahim, told me his wife had been dead eight years, so he was without a wife, like me. But he had two daughters. I asked him who cooked that dinner for me and he said his sister's daughter.

The old dervish wasn't at home, but it was wonderful to walk through the old city, especially wearing my Afghan clothes. I said goodbye to the religious teacher, the sweet, little, humpbacked man, and he blessed my departure and journey, and prayed I'd return. Abdul's sister came to the door unveiled and invited me to tea, but I refused, feeling embarrassed at being with an Afghan woman, and perhaps putting her reputation in jeopardy.

Great clouds are over the city and I don't doubt my departure will coincide with natural events.

I stopped into a shoe store and nearly bought a pair of suede shoes, but the pointy toes threw me off, and the stiffness that I knew would make blisters. The boy in the shoe store didn't mind in the least my trying on shoes with bare, dusty feet. He said all Afghans had dirty feet. A girl was in the store with her veil thrown back off her face—she was a girlfriend of one of the boys and a student. I asked her why she wore a veil and she said her father made her. A boy said that having girlfriends was possible now, but when he asked if everyone in America had a girlfriend and I answered "if they want," I felt in his reaction that a girlfriend here was still not easy to have. Another asked me why America makes war and I told him all governments try to increase their power and influence and if they have guns they use them, that many of us were against the war but had no power to stop it.

At the local post office I said goodbye to the director. There are some people you just naturally love and he's one of them. Standing in the middle of the post office, we kissed a couple of times tearfully. The men there were asking me about prices in New York if they should go— of course, everything sounds astronomical to them. Actually, living in New York isn't so expensive once you know how to shop. But visiting there?

I've made no real friends here and it's my own fault. And with all my frantic searching and bargaining, I didn't buy any rugs. I didn't live in the part of town I love. I never got laid or found a lover. I only scribbled in this diary, and felt foolish.

Irritations: aggressive salesmanship, i.e., looking at a rack of postcards, the salesman will hand you various ones, over-selling the product. Salesmen will call you over—I go politely— and offer you whatever it is they're selling. I say I don't want any and they say Why not? All people asking what time it is, especially irritating when kids call "Mistah"—every kid sometimes— and half will ask the time. But on the other hand many people will stop you to invite you to tea, have melon, smoke hashish, come to dinner.

I notice all sorts of fritters and empanadas being made and sold on the street—I would certainly try them if I'd just arrived, but now am leery with my stomachache. Still, I'm hungry anyway. Yes, I am hungry, a very good sign.

I called the Siceloffs, the Peace Corps family, to say goodbye, and they said Mary has taken Courtney to Pakistan for her teeth.

Dinner at the Tarakis. Fifteen-year-old Joseph picked me up at the hotel in the family car, and on the way to his house we passed a boy and girl out together. He remarked, Well, well, things are certainly changing!

It turned out that Mrs. Taraki is an American from Chicago, and Jewish, so I felt quite relaxed. An American student doing her doctoral thesis on Afghan women was also there. And an American lady named Jean Sulzburger exploring Sufism. Another couple—Afghan man and American woman. And a tourist couple from western North Carolina where they've bought a farm. I was jealous when they talked of the rugs they bought. Two of the women had heard my poetry reading in North Carolina when I was on the circuit there, and one had a copy of my book.

The American grad student has amoebic cysts in her stomach that were discovered when she brought her stool to be analyzed. She didn't have diarrhea so she thought she was all right. Perhaps the cysts are the body's attempt to isolate the germs. But they can break open at any time and then you come down with dysentery. She says some Americans won't go swimming at the Karga Dam outside Kabul because there are dangerous organisms in the water, and you can get sick twenty years later from them. I've been swimming there!

She told the story of a girlfriend of hers traveling in Morocco with a boyfriend, and when they sat with Moroccan men it was always he who was molested. I didn't say anything.

Mr. Taraki told me that Taraki is a tribe near Ghazni and the family have Koochi relatives. He still has Koochi relations dropping in from time to time. He also told me quite a bit about dervishes and dervish houses which he said flourished until the 1880's. A number of them are near Kabul and he said he could have introduced me to the high spiritual leader of one. He also made a few sharp cracks against the King—I knew that's where his son got it from. Poor Joseph, sitting there bored as the adults talked. He seems young for his age. They have a small place, two rooms, in Paghman, but he can't stand it there, so the parents are suffering through the heat of summer in Kabul. Mr. Taraki agreed that Afghanistan was a hard country to live in. Mrs. Taraki has a cousin—a stage designer—in America she can't get to come visit and wants me to persuade him, since she thinks I'm so tuned in here and enthusiastic.

Mr. Taraki repeated a story I'd heard that the Afghanis were descendants of the Israelites, one of the lost tribes. I told him that he seemed very Greek-looking, and he said he has always longed to go to Greece.

I asked about circumcision and was told they do it on the boys around their seventh year, but it can come as late as fifteen, and somebody then said some older men get circumcised too. Among the Uzbek people it's a bigger celebration than marriage.

The grad student says men do feel they have to prove their virility with women here, though, she admits, not to the extent of the western world. She thinks it's that they have their women safely at home and don't have to compete with other men for women.

I should have asked the Tarakis about the changes in Kabul in the last year, for the city has been rapidly growing. And Mrs. Taraki would have had interesting things to say about how the changes applied to women. I should also have asked Mrs. T. about Rosamund Klass whose book on Afghanistan I loved. She said she knew her! Joseph did say that in the last few years there's traffic where there was none before. But the few cars he considers traffic are nothing like what we would consider traffic in the West.

In the car going home I asked the grad student if she turned on and she said Yes, so I gave her my supply, since I couldn't carry it out with me.

AUGUST 13. I'm taking the local bus to the airport. I see thousands of lights strung around the fair grounds for Jeshin. I'm glad to be missing the crowds and the celebration.

It's amazing I haven't been arrested for writing in my book everywhere. Some people look suspicious, but not many are hostile.

The plane is sure to be delayed because of the clouds. The North Carolina couple tried to go to Mazar for three days on an Ariana plane, but it never left. They suggested my flight leaving today was doubtful.

Two months in the country really is barely time to tune in, and I would have been hasty I think to buy rugs and get a lover. Now I think I'm ready, but alas I'm leaving. Mr. Taraki said that since he has no job he could have been helping me a lot, and said I should write him for anything I need—I'd like to ask him to send me some good carpets. A few years ago, he said, guests in Afganistan were given carpets as gifts when they left. He remembers UNESCO visitors got three carpets each. I wonder if you could trust anyone else's taste? I think it might be possible to ask for a typical Baluchi, Mazar, Daulatabad, and Mauri—they seem to be the four main types of rugs here. I can't quite tell the Herat rug that everyone says is not good. Joseph showed me a rug from Khonabad that was too pretty—he said he got it from a friend and the price was $35. I'm always suspicious when the price is quoted in dollars, though. As if to make it seem cheap to the foreigner. The rug was of poor texture and a loose weave.

The view of the city from here shows it clustered at the base of the mountain, which is a view they never photograph. It's more dramatic to photograph it from the mountain above, but since that way the mountain backdrop is cut out, the postcard views of the city are all false. Hills are all around the horizon. It somehow reminds me here of Baraja airport in Madrid, the same bare hills and flat plain.

I had the fantasy there'd be an American soda bar at the airport with malteds and hot dogs, or anyway, grilled ham and cheese sandwiches. But the eggs I'm having are delicious and I see that this is the best breakfast place. I could have come out here to eat. And it's air-conditioned and flyless! And the bus only costs 2 Afs!

One end of the waiting room is all women and children. I walked over there to sit down, caught on to the scene and turned hastily away.

A surprise 20 Afs. tax on domestic flights. First fuck-up—my name wasn't on the list of passengers and they added me to the list as No. 31. I'm sure there'll be no seat.

Some Americans are also going to Herat, carrying picnic lunch boxes from the InterContinental Hotel, but wearing casual clothes. American embassy and military people look so official here among the hippies and Indians and Afghans. No news yet on how long a wait it will be. The Americans are so blasé and cool and distant, there's no talking with them, but immediately I made friends with an Indian boy and an Afghan. The American put-down attitude is horrible. We don't talk to strangers, we don't need friends. Why must Americans be this way?

I talked to a tour guide who works for the Tourist Office and is going to Herat to escort a party of thirty to Kabul. He tells me how easy it is to ship carpets to America—he does it for a lot of tourists. He says I can get an apartment for 200 Afs. a month in Kabul, or a house for 1000 Afs. I was paying 200 a night in the hotel, so of course it was astronomical.

On board. Propeller plane rises slowly—funny feeling after jets. Goodbye Kabul.

I left just in time—I've learned that three thousand Frenchmen are driving from Paris to Kabul in a *rallye* (caravan) of Citroens. They're entering Afghanistan today. Of course it will publicize to the French the possibility of driving to Afghanistan for exotic vacations. So for four days the city will be full of them, and then they head back.

We're making a stop at Mazar-i-Sharif. Mr. Taraki said Ali is not buried at Mazar, he never came near here, so I said if not Ali, a very holy man is buried there, for it has all the vibes. Now my tour guide says only ten percent of the Mazar people are followers of Ali. But there is an eighty percent chance, he says, that it's Ali's tomb.

The plane is filling up at Mazar with a group of French tourists who are going to Herat for a few hours, then flying back, hopefully, to Mazar. This airline has the reputation of breaking down—last week both flights to Herat were cancelled.

I asked my knowledgeable friend why some of the villages had all domed houses and why others were flat roofed. He says domes are cheaper, being mud and straw, whereas flat roofs need wooden beams across. Of course, mud also goes on top finally. He also says the domes are built where there are no earthquakes—there are earthquakes in Kabul, so it has flat roofs, but not in Mazar. I wonder, though, if this is the whole story. He says that's why Ali's tomb can be domed, no earthquakes to wreck it.

There's Balkh out the window, a city designed like a wheel. Was the ancient town also built that way?

The tour guide has two horses, one of which he rents for 1000 Afs. a month. He has a wife and five children, but doesn't have to worry about them if he gets to make a trip to America because his wife's family can take care of them. I guess money isn't the problem in his case. He has many American correspondents who send him gifts.

Behind me are two Sikhs, one of whom has braided sideburns. Their long hair is caught up in their high, peaked turbans. They're not always tall and handsome (or homosexual), as I have heard.

Flying this way over Afghanistan makes it seem almost all desert, except for irrigated rectangles, the green abruptly ending where the irrigation ends. It almost all looks like flying over Utah and Nevada.

Odd what will make my stomach hurt. Breakfast went down fine, but then the tea and cakes served on the plane did it.

Herat. An endless wait for baggage—I haven't yet learned to wait.

And no rooms at the government Herat Hotel with its elegant grounds because of the *rallye*—thousands of French around. I'll have to go to a little dump in town, I guess, probably the Beyzat.

The French love to walk about exotic places dressed in the briefest of bathing suits— they always think it's Club Méditerranée. Their bodies are so muscled and self-conscious. With all these French in town the prices will be way up.

I've just flown over half of Afghanistan and am wasting the day waiting for a bus. It seems that there's no way of going into town for awhile, so I've gone swimming in the hotel pool until the bus from the airport comes by, which will take me into town. I talked to a group of Dutch boys who are traveling together—that really defeats the purpose, it seems to me, of getting to know the people. They say the road to Kabul is closed today and no buses are running because of the *rallye*. They're hoping to get as far as Nepal.

Herat is a noisy little place and has exhausted me. Such a dusty town. The city is full of ruins, rising behind the street fronts. You have to get a little way off to really see them.

I got a room in the new wing of the Beyzat Hotel for 50 Afs., with lots of flies, but otherwise not bad. And bought my bus ticket to leave. Then I headed into the bazaar, innocent that I was. The hustlers descended and though I intended to buy at least the jilak for my mother, they were so aggressive I kept fleeing, and as I fled I was pursued with a desperation that matched mine. One boy on the street selling carpets kept trying to lead me, nudge me, bully me, cajole me, like I was a balky animal. Finally, when he asked me "*Chelozim?*" ("What do you want?), I turned on him, with "You, what do you want?", and he left.

Another man said, "What are you looking for?" and when I furiously answered, "Is it forbidden?" he laughed and invited me to tea. This place only gets transients, so they don't care about being polite, just getting a piece of your money. The carpet trade goes on everywhere and there are very handsome rugs about—everybody seems to be buying and selling them. The copper pot section is hammering from all sides, and I visited weavers of silk *lunghis*. There is actually a lot to buy if they would let you browse and enjoy it. The kids here say "hello goodbye" instead of "Mistah." Some just say "goodbye."

I bought an enamel bowl for yoghurt, and a spoon. I can live on yoghurt, if that's all there is. Now if I can only find some yoghurt to eat with my new dish.

I'm sitting in the filthy restaurant of the old Beyzat Hotel, why I don't know, and have ordered an omelet and potatoes. I spoke with some local teachers at my table. They earn only 1300 Afs. a month and one of them has a wife and two children. But he probably lives in his father's house. His father is an official in the Customs House and has three wives, so he must be rich.

One of the teachers sings on the radio and at weddings, but says there's no theater here. And no *khanega*, although you can never be sure—people really don't know about such things generally.

AUGUST 14. They were busy putting down a macadam surface on the main street in the night, but thanks to Mme. Hashish I slept deeply.

Last night I came back to the hotel and ate a melon, and made friends with some of the French boys of the *rallye* who are staying in the old branch of the Beyzat next door. One, a boy of twenty, was attracted to me and we had our own intimate conversation of the eyes. When I went to my room, coming back to the bathroom, he was lingering in the hall and I got his address. He's driving a Deux Chevaux. How I wish he were going my way.

There must have been a lot of publicity about the *rallye*, for there have been tremendous crowds all along the way – the French are celebrities. I can imagine how the French papers have built it up. When I told the French boys last night that they were pioneers for commercial tourism, a few of them were annoyed, I could tell. I suppose they like to think of themselves as idealists. Whenever the French leave their country, it's like setting off on an expedition into the wilds. They think suitable dress is the briefest of shorts, and arm themselves with a contract from Gallimard to write about their adventures. My only hope is that the French assault on Afghanistan improves the cuisine.

At breakfast, three Pakistani students taking a vacation trip to Turkey with knapsacks say that Farsi and Urdu are very closely related and anyone speaking Farsi should have no trouble with Urdu.

Now to the bus, to the border, westward. I ought to be able to sum up my stay in Afghanistan, say something significant, but I can't—I'm empty. I just want to go on to the next stop and then to the next. One thing, it was nice to be in a country where men go gray young like me.

My main feeling is annoyance that the bus will leave late, anxiety about the border formalities, will everyone have knocked off for hours—for lunch, prayer, siesta? I will get to Mashad very late tonight, I know.

There are two buses going this morning. I'm in the second and I imagine the other will leave sooner and get there sooner. A horrible thought—the other bus is full so it leaves and my bus can't leave until they fill up all the seats.

A religious man across the aisle of the bus is reading from a holy book aloud to his friend. He uses his middle finger to point to the words like my father does, instead of the index like we do. An American in front of them is reading LeRoi Jones's (Amiri Baraka's) *Home*. Oddly, in Kabul one of the few books I saw were copies of Randall Jarrell's book of essays on poetry. Probably it was used for a USIS course.

The desert is all around the town, and from here, where the bus is already stalled with motor trouble at the main intersection of the town, I can see the dry hills stretching away, not far off.

Miles of desert to the border. Passing domed villages with unusual windmills with wooden sails in brick enclosures. Graves covered with flat stones and perhaps one slab upright. A green village a few miles away where there's water. My seat mate is one of the Pakistani boys at breakfast. He says there's a Sikh mosque in Tehran where one can sleep and have breakfast free. He talks about the hostility toward the hippies for begging and smoking grass in public and lying around stoned. He tells me to go to Swat, the Switzerland of Pakistan, and other historical places that mean nothing to me. I'm thinking I must go to Isfahan on the way through Iran—I don't think I should pass it by.

He says there's great competition between the Pakistani bus companies to attract customers and they're even installing record players and TV sets.

This border must be one of the most difficult and complicated in the world, especially now in August. We arrived at eleven o'clock, handed in our passports, and were told to come back at two. There's a little man who stamps the passports, but he has closed himself in his office. There's a sly man who brings him in the passports to stamp for a fee. Then we'll still need the Customs Police to stamp it again. Right now I'm trying to get back my vaccination certificate. But why they should check these when you are leaving the country, I can't imagine.

Meanwhile, it's a hot, barren outpost and a dreary prospect. I think I'd better go try to get the little man to do my passport, for nothing will be done without some action. The next time, I'd better fly.

After standing by the door to the passport office for an hour, with people walking in there through the crowd and coming out mysteriously with passports to hand out to lucky people, I approached a man who had a list of names and found out that for ten Afs. he gets your passport stamped. So I gave him my name and ten Afs. and waited with a group of Pakistanis. Shortly afterward, he came out with the stamped passports but not mine. My ten Afs. had also been taken in to the passport official, and there was a great discussion about my passport and the problem of getting it stamped. This resulted in the man in charge returning my ten Afs. to me, saying foreigners' passports would be taken care of soon and to wait. My attempt at bribery failed miserably. And the day drags on, waiting for this petty tyrant to stamp my passport.

It seems that inside the passport office, the passports are piled in stacks by countries, and local people are taken care of first—of course they have the bribery system set up.

I wonder if I should try to send in my magic letter.

I handed in my letter by the soldier, but he brought back a message that the official was saying his prayers now. I wonder if I will ever see it again. When the door opened, I saw my passport lying on the window ledge and tried to get the soldier to give it to me but he wouldn't. The only thing to do now is wait patiently. I dread spending the night here, but some people have and are still waiting. Oddly, other people get through quickly. Perhaps there are other routes of bribery than the one I took. It does seem it's largely

Americans left here in the waiting room.

Between the Customs House and the Passport Office across the road is a grassy circle with flowers around a flagpole. The travelers have a tendency to cut across the circle to save steps and a path has been worn across it. A soldier is stationed by the flagpole especially to keep people from crossing, but he wasn't there and I cut across. Perhaps he goes to lunch. I was going to the teahouse where a group of local musicians was making marvelous music. I realized that even this border was not a place to be scorned, and if one were stuck here it would be possible to enjoy oneself. It's a dreary desert outpost, but as good as anyplace else.

I notice how westerners stick together in this part of the world and form a club against the "natives." And as long as I'm with Americans and English and French it's painful to go through these frustrating hold-ups of officialdom, but being with the Afghans it is so pleasant. They don't fight it, and are exquisitely charming and friendly. The soldier stationed outside the passport office was imperturbable, an Uzbek from Mazar—he never lost his temper in the crush as he had to push through the crowd and often move them away from the door, no easy task. I spoke with him, and again felt how delicious people from Mazar are.

I keep meeting people who were with me on the bus when I came to Afghanistan, for they keep asking questions about my friend, Sylvaine, the French girl.

Miracle. Again my magic letter worked. The door opened, and a man called me into the Inner Sanctum. My hand was shaken all around and my passport rescued and the exit stamp stamped in. I shook everyone's hand again and walked out delirious into the poor crowd of foreigners waiting there hopelessly. Then I walked across the road to Customs and got the officer to stamp me. I spoke to him, a sweet, tired, overworked man who gets to go home to Herat every fifteen or twenty days.

Then I was finished. The first bus has already left, deserting its foreigner passengers, and I suggested to some French left behind that they try bribery like the Pakistanis did—make a list of names, collect ten Afs. a person, and send someone in with it.

The officials have moved the desks outside and the foreigners have swarmed around them, so perhaps things are getting done. It turned out that one of the problems is that the passport workers can't read or write Western script so they leave those for last. If more and more tourists come here, the border situation will get even worse. We've been here four-and-a-half hours already and we're still not ready to leave, though the worst is over for me. The Iranian border is not this bad, I remember.

I met one of the Pakistanis who helped bribe a health official for 300 Afs. to let some people out without their final cholera shots. But I fear they will be detained at the Iranian border.

It's four o'clock and we've left at last, everyone aboard including those left behind by the first bus. At the last checkpoint at the actual frontier, a soldier is looking at everyone's papers one more time to make sure. Four boys lack the police officer's signature and must go back. The soldier did not accept an offer of money. Luckily, it's a short walk.

Now after an hour's ride, we're across the border and at Iranian customs, but the bus to Mashad leaves at five and I don't see how we'll make it, if the road from now on is as bad as I remember it. Perhaps a taxi or jeep or minibus will be there to take us.

Iran immediately seems modern to me. A new asphalt road has been put in to the border so we ride along smoothly. Officials are swift and polite. At the border I change some money, buy a Pepsi, amaze everyone with my Farsi. I notice how different the accent is -- the difference between Farsi as the Iranians speak it and as the Afghans speak it is the difference between an English accent and an American. The Iranians sound elegant with their drawled A's, very English in fact.

From Mashad, where this diary began, I was able to take a train to Teheran, and from there, a so-called "luxury" bus to Tabriz in western Iran, where I realized that I was quite ill and wondered "if this cold I have is all the sickness of Afghanistan coming out of me." After another difficult border crossing into Turkey, and a harrowing minibus ride around the base of Mt. Ararat to Erzurum, I took a train to Kayseri in the center of Turkey, from where I could get to a port with a boat or a plane to Cyprus and from there to Israel, where I'd have a friend, medical care, good food, and time to recover.

AUGUST 20. On the train through Turkey I slept quite well, though as usual lately I got up at five. When time changes, the one thing the body's timer can go by is the dawn.

We're going through an almost barren landscape of rocky mountains and sparse pasture, a cultivated valley here and there—so much of where I've been has been like this. But the trees are different and the elegant irrigation canals don't seem to exist here.

A large family is sharing my compartment, and Mama has so much energy she dominates the family scene—she certainly bustles about, doing all the work. And of course the men depend on her. She told me in a burst of friendliness that though she worked as a teacher and her husband was the head of the PTT, they didn't make enough money and were going to Germany to look for work. I told them life in Germany was very expensive. They didn't even know what city they were heading for.

I've spent hours in the dining car having breakfast, mostly talking with a radical young Turkish mining engineer. He was in the military academy when fifteen hundred of the officer-trainees were expelled some years ago for left-wing activities. He says that ten families control fifty-six percent of Turkish wealth. Turkey has vast iron ore reserves and the government is criminal for importing iron ore for its new steel mill. One of the crooked deals involved forces them to pay high prices for shipping the ore in foreign vessels—since Turkey doesn't have that kind of ships—so it will be expensive steel. The most profitable type of mining was building materials—sand, cut stone— and there was small investment. He considered the Saudis the stupidest people alive, because their monarch, Faisal, owns all the oil personally and does what he wants with it, and while they're desperately poor, he gives each of his wives a Cadillac.

He hates the U.S. government and admires China the most. He thinks the moon exploration is a waste of money when there are so many needs on earth. He doesn't know why America was buying up iron ore reserves of 20 percent iron which is uneconomic to mine. He even told me where the American airfields were in Turkey, one in Adana on the Mediterranean coast where I'm going, and said most people don't know about them because the American soldiers aren't allowed into town.

I asked him if he had a good life in Ankara where he lived, and he said no, life was too anxious to be a pleasure. He and his friends are watched by police and their mail opened, so it's a paranoid scene. The government had killed the leading labor leader, and Istanbul is still under Martial Law with

185 students in jail. When I asked for his address in Ankara he gave me his work address, saying he had no home address. I felt he wasn't opposed to making out with me, although the extreme left wing always has conflicts about this.

His English is excellent—a rare thing, for he attended an American College in Ankara. He'd like to go to the Colorado College of Mines and get his Ph.D., but a friend of his had been turned down because he was a Muslim when he applied to a church college. I told him one turn-down means nothing—you should make a hundred applications.

He thinks there's a strong possibility of my getting a boat from Adana to Cyprus. He had friends who went that way. I can't wait to get to the sea and breathe that air. But he says that the Black Sea shore is more beautiful and peaceful than the Mediterranean coast and the water less salty. People go into the dunes of Mersin and smear themselves with honey and bake in the sun for a few hours—then they don't wash for three days. This is supposed to cure aches and pains. I'm sure that after walking around sticky and sandy for three days, it's like bliss to wash off!

When he tried to pay for my breakfast, I insisted on paying for his. Then he said, a little shocked, "But you're the guest!" I laughed and said, "Not guest, imperialist." He grew quite romantic at parting for he said, "Give my greetings to the young of America." Now why does that seem theatrical? A young Lenin might have said it. This boy might be the young Lenin of Turkey. I find it a moving statement, yet I smile.

A woman came into the dining car who for a moment I thought was the woman in my compartment and I flashed a smile at her, then immediately realized my mistake. She was quite angry, for you don't smile at strange ladies in this part of the country, and in fact it could be the cause of murder. The women are largely unveiled, but nothing else is really changed. And there was no way to explain or apologize, so I hoped it would pass over, and it did. Luckily, tempers flare quickly but briefly here.

Outside Kayseri, in the flat valley below a snow-capped mountain, are vast sunflower fields, with beehives set around them to make sunflower honey. Lots of big, fat marijuana plants are growing on the edges of cultivated fields. We passed a village of cave dwellers and earth dwellers. Each house had an arched stone entrance, like to a subway. It's almost a California valley. Great stacks of sunflower heads lie by the road. Fruit seems very cheap, even cheaper than in Afghanistan. Another snow-capped mountain lies between Kayseri and the sea.

From the station I took a carriage into town, which is being totally rebuilt. Kayseri has a famous bazaar of carpets and is the central market for southern Turkey, especially for silk carpets. The bazaar is among the old ruined walls and buildings, so it has a lot of atmosphere. A charming young student of twenty took me around. He wasn't just practicing his English on me either. The city doesn't get many tourists and the merchants practically tackle you. But I wasn't impressed by the silk carpets. Still, Turkish carpets succeed by their gaiety even if they're garish. I asked about foreigners in Kayseri and was told that they were tourists visiting caves nearby and there's also a NATO airbase with Persian pilots.

The bus trip from Kayseri to the coast is supposed to take five hours. Among the dry brown peaks of the mountains, one is green—it looks like it could be a volcano. This land is very ancient. You feel there are buried cities everywhere. A village in the distance with strange, tall houses like Thucydides described in *The Anabasis*. Another troglodyte village with the same simple stone archway over the entrance. Peach trees heavy with enormous fruit, vineyards, and at last the first, silvery, olive trees. It's good to be back to olive trees.

I had to feign sleep for awhile because a man across the aisle of the bus insisted on shouting at me in Turkish to make me understand. He comes from a tiny mountain hamlet outside of Kayseri with only a dirt track. He's sweet and has blue eyes and I was afraid he was getting annoyed by my incomprehension, because he was hitting my shoulder harder and harder to make me understand. Luckily, a great peasant woman squeezed in next to him, blocking him off. But then she moved to the back of the bus and I was at the mercy of my shouting mountain Turk again. I kept saying I didn't understand. Only sleep ended it.

You can't help but build up sexual tension on a bus with your seat mate. It always happens. I'm getting definite vibes from mine.

AUGUST 21. It's strange, but every place I've been on my way home has been thrilling.

Last night, more dead than alive, I woke from a doze to find that the bus driver had decided to skip Mersin, the port on the coast where I was hoping to get off, probably because he was behind schedule, and drove straight to Adana. I'd looked forward to the sea, and here I was in an inland city. At the bus station on the outskirts of Adana, there was a car going to Mersin if it ever got enough passengers, but it looked hopeless, so I lugged my valise that seemed to have turned to stone down the road, not being able to make anyone understand that I wanted to go to the town center or to a good hotel. Suddenly I saw orange trees with green fruit, and there were bananas on fruit stands and big lemons. The air had a humid, balmy Florida weight to it. I started feeling better and accepted this change in my itinerary.

I came to a square full of outdoor restaurants, making the city look very gay. A handsome officer led me to a hotel that looked all right—cheesily modern, which is often a trap. The hotel manager who is bald has let his back hairs grow very long and pasted them with lacquer across his forehead, giving the impression of a bad toupee. He's an unpleasant, unfriendly man. Sick and tired from the bus, as I was, he didn't greet me or act kindly, and then tried to palm off on me an airless back room, first floor rear. I've learned to be quite suspicious. People tell you what they want to, to get what they want out of you or to get you to do what they want. In Erzerum, all the street hustlers kept insisting the hotel, where we finally got rooms, was filled up, trying to get us to go to their hotels. At the restaurant, the waiter said he would give us 14 Tl to the dollar and when I told him the bank gave 14.85 he said it wasn't true. In the train, the dining car waiter offered only 10. At the Turkish border a man said there was no bus all the way through to Erzerum, but I'm sure if I hadn't settled for the minibus to Agri, a regular bus to Erzerum would have turned up. But sometimes, when tired, I fall for it, like when the railroad clerk said there wasn't any wagon light on the train to Kayseri.

Now in spite of feeling wrecked, I turned down the dark hole of a room and he gave me my nice room. It costs 30 Tl. (Turkish lira), which seemed a lot at first until I realized it was only $2. It has an overhead fan, far superior to air conditioning. And a bathtub! I climbed in and soaked, blessing my luck. Then I went out for an hour, ate some yoghurt, went to Turkish Airlines and got on the waiting list for the plane to Cyprus tomorrow afternoon—the clerk said there was a 90 percent chance of getting on. Arming myself with bananas, a lemon, half a watermelon, codeine and morphine pills for my cold, and more yoghurt, I'm back in my room. If I feel well enough in the morning, I'll go to the Roman ruins which has a bridge surviving from Roman times. And if I don't get on the plane I'll go to Mersin and see about a boat.

This city is a lot like Tampa, with a lot of shabby streets and a few boulevards of fancy high-rise buildings, not as many palm trees but the same oleanders and flowers growing in profusion with no special care. It's the first place I've been all summer where there's no need for irrigation.

The women here walk around in harem pajamas, gathered at waist and ankle. Some middle-aged women look like big, gypsy women. The old men are especially warm and beautiful. A lot of people make disapproving sounds over my hair—I lost patience with one young man and snapped at him that I didn't care what he thought and moved on. On the bus last night my pesty neighbor across the aisle went through the number of pointing to the women and then at the men, saying no man but me had long hair, only the women.

I keep remembering a strange man in the bus serail at Tehran. He was like a hermaphrodite. He had the smooth, though slightly wrinkled, face of a boy, or a woman dressed in man's clothes. He might have been a woman trying to pass as a man, who'd cut her hair like a man's, though his body seemed quite all right. This was really the only inter-sex type I saw in the East. The other men knew about him, I guess, because they were reaching for his crotch repeatedly and he fended them off, giggling. It turned sick when one tough man started giving him judo chops to the head and neck and he almost fell. Another man said he was "schweine"— the usual reaction of the world to someone different.

People in Adana know more about the world's geography, perhaps because of the American installation. When I say I'm from the U.S. they don't get confused. One man, when I said I was American, even asked if I was Mexican. A nice old man who sold me fruit said I had a Turkish face. I can really pass for anything except as a U.S. citizen.

Sundown. All the muezzins are calling the faithful to prayer, sounding like cantors. The Jews and Muslims are so close—both say Peace to you as a greeting. The music is very similar. They both circumcise. The same traditions about money.

AUGUST 22. I just got up having slept 18 hours and am somewhat better.

A nice restaurant owner stands outside his restaurant snaring customers. He snared me by saying he had chicken soup, but it doesn't taste like chicken soup. Everybody is having soup and bread for breakfast. I didn't have the strength to walk to the old town and bought some peaches from a pleasant old man and came back to my room. I looked at myself clearly in the mirror for the first time and I'm terribly thin.

Now I'm sitting in a garden terrasse having a glass of ayran, the yoghurt drink, which tastes like Milk of Magnesia to me. The air is so good here in Adana. A pity I wasn't able to get to the seashore. There's a big marijuana plant growing on the flower border of a cafe right by the public gardens nearby. This neighborhood is the usual Miramar neighborhood where the fortunate few in a poor country get to live.

There are a great number of young men about, but I'm not getting any vibes of interest. And even though they're lean and handsome they don't turn me on. I see one longish-haired boy. Some of them walk arm-in-arm, but there's little handholding in this neighborhood. They wear trim pants—no bell bottoms here yet—and crisp shirts. They're dressed like American boys a few years ago. Even here, though, a number of men and boys are wearing Turkish baggy drawers.

In this part of the world all the horses seem to have big balls. You hardly ever see a mare.

Nicosia, Cyprus. There were plenty of seats on the plane, as it turned out. I hooked up with two British soldiers who were returning from leave in Turkey. One of them said about the Turks crowding around the airline desk for tickets, "These people will not form queues." I pointed out that only the English do.

I had to take another cholera shot on entering Cyprus. Apparently the one I got in Tehran wasn't enough, but in the Middle East where the epidemic rages, no doctor said anything. Many of the arrivals were getting their first one.

I've found an expensive hotel with a charmer of a landlady, short and shapeless with a balding head. Her expression was so human that I forgave her for soaking me.

Nicosia is a lot like Palma de Majorca except that it's divided and barricaded like Berlin with U.N. soldiers patrolling the border. I walked down the street along a battle-scarred area between the opposing halves of the city, until I noticed I was the only pedestrian and it might be dangerous.

The side of town I'm in is all being rebuilt modern, but it doesn't feel Greek. The Cypriot soldiers wear tight, brief pants, the most revealing I've ever seen outside the U.S. Navy. There are few tourists, and the Greeks seem to ignore me. Perhaps the clue lies in what the British soldiers answered when I asked if they'd learned Greek. "We never mix," they said. Perhaps there is a policy of mutual ignoring.

Everybody in this town seems to be stuffing sweets into his mouth as fast as he can. I too am succumbing and have just had what they call a strawberry milkshake that is nothing of the kind. I have no idea what things cost. I turned $10 into Cypriot money and think I'll have enough until I depart for Israel. The Cypriot pound is divided into innumerable somethings and there are several kinds of coins in the same denomination. So I've given up.

My bones are sticking out like they haven't for fifteen years.

Tomorrow morning I'll be able to get a flight to Israel.

AUGUST 23. I was awakened in the night by the sound of revelers and realized I was back in the Christian world and it's Saturday night. This area is full of cabarets which perhaps is a euphemism for places to pick up call girls.

The plane to Israel is almost empty. Most of the passengers seem to be a group of elderly Americans with their ebullient tour guide. It's ridiculously expensive, $68, for such a short flight, but that's always the case with international flights. I can see hills of what I think is Lebanon off to the left of the plane.

It's terribly moving for a Jew to arrive in Israel, one's ancestral land. I said to myself that all these people are mine—the fat lady who looked like she was a good comic, and the glamorous young man who belonged on the beach at St. Tropez and the short fat man with the diamond pinkie ring holding a cigar. But it's hard to keep the feeling of "sacred land" while going through customs formalities, especially if you have a gurgling stomach ache. The mini skirts here must be the shortest in the world this side of Tahiti. Suddenly I'm in the modern world—an air-conditioned terminal I never want to leave. Ice cream on a stick covered with chocolate! The terminal being enlarged in two directions. You feel technology grasped and used.

Israel, the only country in the Near and Middle East where no man wears a jacket, where dress is as informal as possible. In the English language newspaper there was even a letter to the editor that complained that TV newscasters dress too formally, setting a bad example.

I talked with an Afghan boy who came from Herat. His one grievance against Israel was that here the family was split up, with some off in the army, even his sister!, and different branches living separately, whereas in Herat they all lived in one house of twenty rooms.

Israel means medical care, which I desperately needed, and I managed to stagger to my friend, Robert Friend's house in Jerusalem and there collapsed. He was alarmed by my skeletal state and sent for the doctor who diagnosed a deep bronchial infection, close to pneumonia, and gave Robert instructions and prescriptions. I'm sinking into his loving attentions.

What do I think now of Afghanistan? I can hardly believe I was there or remember what it was like. Was one of its main charms that everything was so cheap? My main regret—that I didn't buy carpets, all I was allowed.

Everything I tell Robert about Afghanistan confirms him in his feeling that it's an awful place he'd never want to go to. It's true—I think of the terrible food, the flies, etc.—yet it was so much more and that's what I don't think I'll be able to convey to anyone.

Edward Field's collections of poetry include *Counting Myself Lucky* (Black Sparrow) and *After the Fall: Poems Old and New* (Pittsburgh University Press). His nonfiction book, *The Man Who Would Marry Susan Sontag, and Other Intimate Literary Profiles of the Bohemian Era*, is now available from University of Wisconsin Press, and he has co-written several novels with Neil Derrick. He resides in New York City.

Made in the USA
San Bernardino, CA
08 February 2015